MW00623592

Walking in the Resurrection

Walking in the Resurrection

Myron S. Augsburger

Introduction by
Keith Miller

HERALD PRESS
Scottdale, Pennsylvania
Kitchener, Ontario
1976

Library of Congress Cataloging in Publication Data

Augsburger, Myron S
Walking in the Resurrection.

Includes bibliographical references.
1. Christian life — Mennonite authors. I. Title.
BV4501.2.A93 248'.48'97 76-15566
ISBN 0-8361-1333-0

WALKING IN THE RESURRECTION

Published simultaneously in Canada by Herald Press, Kitchener, Ont. N2G 4M5
Library of Congress Catalog Card Number: 76-15566
International Standard Book Number: 0-8361-1333-0
Printed in the United States of America
Design: Alice B. Shetler

To Mr. and Mrs. Peter Leuenberger of Basel, Switzerland, whose gracious spirit and hospitality reflected the new life in Christ and enabled me, with Esther and Marcia, to spend an enjoyable time in Switzerland in study and research.

CONTENTS

INTRODUCTION

Where have the people gone?

During the past few years thousands of Christians have become disillusioned with the institutional church. Some have left to join humanistic social action ventures. Others have simply disappeared into the secular world where they felt they could find a style of living at least less hypocritical and impersonal than they saw life in the church to be.

But a fresh breeze has been blowing through the church during these same years. Men and women have begun to see the gospel in terms of *living* it in the different *relationships* of their lives — rather than primarily in terms of abstract doctrinal statements or individual piety. This "relational" approach to theology has brought thousands of people into (or back into) a vital relationship with Jesus Christ and with other Christians. It is concrete and deals with life.

In *Walking in the Resurrection* Myron Augsburger describes a way of living relationally which, it seems to me, includes many of the healthiest aspects of the various renewal movements.

The "honesty" of life in the resurrection is not a new legalism but springs from God's acceptance of our unadorned confession and repentance. As we live together as children of the same Father, His purposes,

His will may become ours. We are motivated not by fear but as a natural result of an emerging awareness of the awesome and specific love of God for us and for each person everywhere.

Walking in the Resurrection is a strong statement calling for a Christian ethic based on relationships with Christ and His people, rather than on rigid rules. Questions concerning political and social involvement, the use of money and power, war and peace, which evangelical Christians have often avoided or repressed are shown to be integrally involved in the life and ministry of the person who walks in the resurrection.

For veteran church people who have not been involved in this more relational approach to Christian living, the clear, seemingly unambiguous life of commitment and servanthood may appear to be naive and utopian. And if life in this fellowship did not include the *continuing* and *renewing* process of repentance, confession, and forgiveness, it would be utopian.

But the pages which follow present a clear, gutsy call to the Spirit and life of Jesus to a world and a church filled with clouded statements and plastic models. I feel challenged by Myron Augsburger to move beyond my own provincial, individualistic boundaries toward the broader mainstream of secular history where people are lost from the lack of Christ and His life in the resurrection.

Keith Miller
Port Aransas, Texas

AUTHOR'S PREFACE

In Christian thought there is need for clear understanding on the meaning of reconciliation as a central aspect of the Christian experience. Reconciliation with God in Christ results in a reconciliation between the believer and his brother in society.

Reconciliation must be thought of in terms of both salvation and peace. Salvation means the end of one's rebellion against God and the beginning of a new fellowship of joy with Him. It also means the end of isolation from others and the beginning of a new relationship with one's fellowman.

The new life in Christ, or the resurrection life, is a quality of life expressing to the world the victory Jesus Christ has won over the powers of darkness. In the Christian faith we need to demonstrate adequately both the objective and subjective aspects of relationship with Christ.

This book seeks to show how one's relationship with Christ, by His indwelling Spirit, transforms one's life and fellowship with others. It also attempts to show how genuine evangelical faith issues in a social consciousness and responsibility.

Holiness of life is not a pious exercise apart from practical responsibilities, but is wholeness of life in relation to Christ, to oneself, and to one's fellowman. My purpose in writing *Walking in the Resurrection* is to give a clear expression of the transforming power of the Christian faith "that in all things he might be glorified."

Myron S. Augsburger
March 3, 1976

The CENTRALITY of CHRIST

1

The Centrality of Christ

"Like as Christ was raised up from the dead by the glory of the Father, even so we also should walk in newness of life" (Romans 6:4, KJV). Often used in the baptismal formula, this statement affirms the new life in Christ.

As a boy of eleven, I stood in a little stream in an open pasture in northwestern Ohio and heard these words quoted by Bishop Ben B. King, who had just baptized me with water. Having received baptism upon my confession of faith, I was expected from that moment forward to remain separated from the life of the old self and to live a new life in the Spirit of Jesus. The congregation of brothers and sisters in the faith stood on the bank witnessing my confession. After I and others baptized with me were welcomed as members of the church, we all joined together in singing God's praise.

During the 3 1/2 decades since, the meaning of that hallowed moment has become a way of life for me. That's what confessing Jesus as Lord is all about—a way of life. To recognize Him as Lord means *walking in the resurrection*.

And that's what this book is all about. What does it mean to live in a world where Jesus Christ is risen, where He is alive and acting, and where He is open for encounter at any moment? What does it mean to share His life, the new life in which we know Christ not after the flesh but after the Spirit? (See 2 Corinthians 5:16.)

How does one come to know, beyond a doubt, a saving relation with God and experience a deep-down release from guilt? And further, what is the character of the new life and the quality of fellowship described as walking in the resurrection?

As Christians we seem obsessed at times with self-examination, introspection, confession of the warped shape of our personalities, analysis of causes, and attempting to discover what our "naked" self is really like. When all is said and done, we finally admit to ourselves and to others what we claimed to have confessed to God at our baptism — that we are sinners — ugly, selfish, miserable sinners. Why should we express surprise when we discover some blemish in our lives? Apart from Christ, we are rotten to the core. Far too often we have assumed ourselves to be quite good and find it difficult to admit our perversions.

But such candidness is only the starting place for a satisfactory experience. Once we are honest about our aggressions, our lust, our bitterness, our angers — what next? A measure of peace comes to one who no longer hides his sins from himself, who no longer spends his psychic energies suppressing guilt, it is true. But this is not the new life in Christ. It may be only a psychological game of self-affirmation in which I say "hello" to myself as I really am rather than continuing to practice self-deception about who I want to project myself to be. Or at best it may be a step of repentance, a gesture toward the new life, but it is only a step.

Identification with Christ brings a totally new orientation into one's life. Rather than being obsessed with our self-awareness we come to a Christ-awareness in which the deepest level of the soul cries out, "He is my Lord, He is my Master, I will to be like Him!" This must become our conscious affirmation we experience the bursting forth of a new life, the life of the resurrection.

Much has been written in recent years on the centrality of Christ. We have been confronted anew with the historic Jesus, with the acts of God in history, with the concept of saving history (*Heilsgeschichte*), with the revelation of God in Christ, and with what it means to be truly human. But this renewal of emphasis on the importance of Jesus Christ must be carried further. There has been too little discussion and awareness of the new life in relation to the risen Christ. There is need for an additional chapter expressing the relation of Christ to the believer's life and thus to ethics, interpreting the meaning of walking with Jesus as Master and Lord.

This emphasis on the new life is directly related to the resurrection. As Gerhard Delling says, "Without the resurrection of Christ, there would be no reconstituting of human life and existence by God, and the whole of man's life and existence is always implied here . . . inseparable from making it possible for man to walk in a new way."[1] Early Christians regarded the raising of Jesus from the dead as the decisive act of God's saving work. Paul affirms in 2 Corinthians 13:14 that he lived only through the risen Christ, in the power of God expressed in Jesus' resurrection. Similarly Peter links the freedom of a clear conscience with the resurrection. (See 1 Peter 3:21.) The true Christian disciple participates in a spiritual transformation which supplies the power for a new life, for the highest ethical behavior. We do not simply adopt a new ethical code and try to live by it.

Many persons admire the ethical teachings of Jesus but want to separate them from His claim of Savior and Lord. This sets up a false dichotomy. For example, confronted with Jesus' pacifism, some persons want to be pacifists but are not sure they want to be Christians! Others want Jesus as their Savior. In spite of His teachings on pacifism, they are sure they want to be Christians but not pacifists. However, the moral and religious teaching of Jesus must be held together. As T.W. Manson says, "To divorce the moral teaching of Jesus from His teaching as a whole is thus to make it practically useless; it is to make it unintelligible." [2]

One evidence that the emphasis on Jesus has been too limited is the resurgence of the charismatic, the widespread interest in an experiential relationship with the Holy Spirit. This movement has given a more modern existential character to the historic emphasis of the personal knowledge of the Holy Spirit, of the indwelling of the Spirit, the infilling of the Spirit. Yet, wonderful as this experience is, it needs constant identification with Jesus. Otherwise, it becomes a mere pietistic revival without the obedience, the discipleship, the responsibilities of love Jesus demands. I'm reminded of the story of a man who prayed, "Fill me, Lord, fill me." A brother kneeling beside him broke in, "You can't do it, Lord. He leaks!" That's why we need to share in a more complete way the life of Jesus Christ, to identify with Him each day, to begin walking in the resurrection.

This emphasis is one of the unique aspects of the Swiss Brethren faith in the sixteenth century (or Anabaptists, as they were called). They were not a group of social or political reformers, but people of a simple, yet profound faith in the lordship of the risen Christ. Their concept of a believers' church held that those truly converted to Christ are bound together in a new life, in a covenant of love and responsibility. They spoke of the believers as "born again," as walking in the Spirit, as experiencing a new life in contrast to the old. This life they described as following Christ, or discipleship.

The belief of the Anabaptists was directly related to how they interpreted the Scriptures. They found in the fullness of the revelation of Christ the key to understanding salvation history.[3] They saw revelation as the process of God's self-disclosure. They found in the Bible two levels of revelation. The Old Testament relates to the New as promise relates to fulfillment. They recognized an unfolding revelation in which the ultimate Word is Christ Himself. We now interpret the Bible through Christ. The Incarnation is final. We do not base interpretations of Christian doctrine or ethics on the Old Testament without first interpreting them through the full revelation of Christ.

Further, this Christ-oriented emphasis gives us our

only sure knowledge of what God is like. While God is introduced to us throughout the Old Testament in His acts of self-disclosure, He is fully known only in Jesus Christ. God is like Jesus. Jesus said, "He who has seen me has seen the Father" (John 14:9). Some persons in their philosophical quest try to "go behind Jesus" to understand God. But this attempt gives us a God without a face. It limits us to philosophical concepts of ultimate good, or of an ultimate Being, but provides no meaningful relation with God. In Christ we are reconciled to a personal God whom we can now address as "our Father." And in the forgiveness and fellowship of the risen Christ we share a new quality of life.

Our relationship with the risen Christ keeps our discipleship from becoming legalistic. The emphasis on following Christ keeps our experience from becoming merely pietistic. This Anabaptist concept of discipleship undergirds my own faith, and calls me again and again to discover the real meaning of living with Christ, of walking in the resurrection.

The resurrection of Christ is directly related to the new life open to the believer. (See Romans 6:4.) In their new existence Christians take part in the resurrection of Jesus. Paul related the resurrection of Jesus directly to the justification of the believer. "Jesus . . . was put to death for our trespasses and raised for our justification" (Romans 4:25). The resurrection life is the new humanity Jesus is creating in us by His Spirit. We are called to share His purpose for us by conscious participation, willing the will of Christ.

On several occasions I have stood and gazed at

Rembrandt's painting of "The Emmaus Road" and wished that I could have heard the words of the risen Christ. Yet I have met Him in thought and in the spirit. I find that life can be an Emmaus Road, where the risen Lord confronts me again and again. But we meet Christ only in faith. When we fail to reach out to Him in belief, we miss the fellowship of the risen Christ. This emphasis may be illustrated by Rembrandt's approach to His biblical subject matter. While many of his fellow artists were obsessed with Christ's birth and death, Rembrandt concentrated on His life, His deeds, and His lordship. His painting of the Nativity was set in a contemporary home. His scenes of Jesus include the washing of the disciples' feet. The Emmaus Road appearance of Christ carries us beyond His descent from the cross. So in our experiences of Christian faith, the way in which people describe their experience of Christ depends upon their perspective.

The perspective of this book calls for confessing the lordship of the risen Christ, of being led by the Spirit of Jesus, of walking in the resurrection. We must move beyond the experience of salvation and participate in the ongoing life of God. Believing is behaving in relationship. It is a covenant with the Master, certified with His own blood. Whenever we observe the Lord's Supper, we covenant with Him, to the death, to participate actively in His kingdom. We pledge to do this "until he comes" (1 Corinthians 11:26), an expression of our faith in the triumph of our Lord and of the ultimate fulfillment of His kingdom. As the kingdoms of history come and go, as they decay or fall or change to another kingdom, we stand amidst the crumbling empires and join the heavenly host saying, "The kingdom of the world has become the kingdom of our Lord and of his Christ, and he shall reign for ever and ever. . . . Hallelujah! For the Lord our God the Almighty reigns" (Revelation 11:15; 19:6). This participation by faith with Christ in His ultimate victory is the present identification of the true disciple.

I have been made aware again and again of my own failures to appropriate the resurrection power. Intellectually, I have seen enough to give me sincere appreciation, even exhilaration, over the quality of this partnership with Christ. But emotionally, and socially, I am so vulnerable to the pressures of my own moods, feelings, and biases. My determination to live the gospel calls me to my knees before the Master. Only in Him do I find the resurrection power to live the new life.

The gap between teaching and doing is expressed in an interesting story. Two men went to the temple to pray — the one, a successful businessman; the other a poor schoolteacher. The businessman stood and prayed within himself, "God, I thank you that I am not as other men are, especially as this poor schoolteacher here. I'm a member of the board of trustees where he teaches. I'm chairman of the salary committee. In fact, I pay half his salary myself." The poor schoolteacher wouldn't so much as lift up his eyes to heaven, but said, "God, be merciful to me, I was that man's teacher."

Chapter 3 of Paul's letter to the Colossians is the classic expression of new life in Christ, a resurrection life. Take time to read it carefully again before you read further in this book. Then pray with St. Ignatius of Loyola: "Take, O Lord, and receive my entire liberty, my memory, my understanding, and my whole will. All that I am, all that I have, You have given me, and I will give it back again to You to dispose of according to Your good pleasure. Give me only Your love and Your grace; with You I am rich enough, nor do I ask for anything besides."

The KNOWLEDGE of GOD

2

The Knowledge of God

Can one know God? This question has puzzled people of every culture and time. Modern thinkers ask, "Can finite humans really know God when He is so completely "other" from us? But persons now and in the past claim to know Him, and this "knowing" has changed their lives. And through their witness, others of us have been brought to Him. In this relationship, God is our Father. Through Him we know what it is "to belong." We know the meaning and satisfaction of life.

God cannot be known as a tree, or a flower, or a bird is known. He is not an object that can be examined as one examines a mineral. To seek physical evidence of the reality of God is to place the idea of God in a sphere which is beneath the realm of proper thought about God. The message of the Bible is that God is Creator and that He stands beyond that which He has created. To identify Him with the creation itself is to think of Him as less than He is.

Paul writes, "For us there is one God, the Father, from whom are all things and for whom we exist, and one Lord, Jesus Christ, through whom are all things and through whom we exist" (1 Corinthians 8:6). To know God one must begin by an affirmation of faith that reaches beyond the things of creation. To know

Him, the Bible says, one "must believe that he exists and that he rewards those who seek him" (Hebrews 11:6). The quest for knowledge of God is not fulfilled by learning some things about Him, but only as we come to Him for Himself.

Jesus prayed to God for all of us who are reaching out for spiritual reality, "That they might know thee the only true God, and Jesus Christ, whom thou hast sent (John 17:3, KJV). This knowledge of God, Jesus said, is eternal life! To know God is to become involved with Him in His goals and eternal program. For us, as creatures of time, this is an opportunity to share the realities of another realm, to participate in His life.

If the knowledge of God is relational, involving the inner spirit of man, does this mean that faith is not rational or informed? To say that God is outside the realm of scientific proof does not mean that there is no evidence for God. In honesty we must admit that scientifically one can neither prove nor disprove God. But neither can we prove love, one of the most wonderful experiences in human relations. Does this cause us to doubt that love exists? Of course not. We accept love on the basis of evidence. Similarly, our faith in God is based on evidence, not on scientific proof.

The greatest evidence is Jesus Christ. He is the most convincing witness in all of human history to the reality of God and to the privilege of knowing Him. Jesus said, "He who has seen me has seen the Father" (John 14:9). God is like Jesus. In Jesus we can find the knowledge of God. The Bible presents God as acting in history, revealing Himself most fully in Jesus Christ, but the Bible does not discuss the Being of God philosophically. We know God through what He had done in history, not by pure philosophical reflection as Plato or Buddha attempted. Oscar Cullmann says, "While the Bible from beginning to end speaks of God's *activity*, and not the *being* of God the Father, Son, and Holy Spirit, nevertheless a Being is revealed *in* this activity."[1]

In our relationships on the human level, we never really know another person until that person reveals himself. Some people live around each other for years without really knowing one another until some crisis causes them to open up. Similarly, we can only know God if He reveals Himself to us. We are dependent upon His revelation. This is a basic aspect of the meaning of faith. We believe, through the evidence of history, that God has acted to reveal Himself.

Through the centuries God gradually revealed more and more of Himself until the supreme act when He came in Jesus Christ. Apart from Jesus it is impossible to have an adequate understanding of God. Karl Barth said, "Either Jesus Christ was God or we don't have a full revelation yet." But at this point we must face the distinction between knowledge *about* God and the knowledge *of* God. Even with the full revelation of God in Jesus Christ, there is constant danger that we read the Bible to gain knowledge *about* Him and fail to come to the knowledge *of* Him.

This was the problem in Israel, which Paul exposes in Romans 9. God calls us through His Word, but it is *His calling us* that is important. The Bible is the medium through which His call comes to us. True, faith is response to His Word, but above all it is response to Him! God spoke to Abraham, the father of God-followers, but God spoke a *word of promise*. The promise made it necessary for Abraham to look to Him in faith. It is important for us to recognize that faith has its historical basis in God speaking a word of promise.

To believe is to respond to the calling of God, to respond to His Word. God called, Abraham answered. God called, Isaac answered. God called Esau and Jacob, Jacob answered. Paul affirms in Romans 9 that we do not experience the knowledge of God simply by being a part of a Christian ethnic group in which God-language is used. We only know God when we hear His call to us and respond in faith. His calling is an opportunity to come to know Him.

Paul transcends ethnic religion. As a blueblood Jew he refers to the fellowship of believers as "us whom he has called, not from the Jews only but also from the Gentiles" (Romans 9:24). This statement sets the new people of God above ethnic identification by distinguishing them as people who hear God's call for themselves. They now share the faith experience of Abraham. They, too, are God-followers.

We can never truly know God just by acquiring intellectual knowledge about His great acts in the past, even His acts in Christ, unless in those acts we hear His call and respond in believing action. Nor can we fully know God by diligently studying the Bible, even though it is God's Word written. The study of the Bible must move us beyond head knowledge about its words and structures to an inner response to His Word of promise. Some of us may master the original languages and understand all the implications of form criticism and yet with all this intellectual knowledge of the Bible not hear God. The legalists among us may memorize texts that call for godly behavior and yet not hear God. We know God only by faith, by the believing attitude that hears Him in His Word of promise and responds to His call. This inner response is the expression of faith, evidence that we are meeting God as Abraham did. Faith is acting on God's call.

But the Bible says we have "a more sure word" in Jesus Christ. (See 2 Peter 1:19, KJV.) The knowledge of God takes form in Jesus of Nazareth. Without this expression of God the experience of hearing Him would be left to impressions that are quite subjective. How does one know that he is truly being called by God and that the inner awareness is not a projection of some psychological need? As we study the life of Jesus Christ, what He was in addition to what He said, we come to understand more fully what God is like. In Jesus, in the form of humanness, we hear the Word of God — not primarily a word of what God is like, not a philosophical word for our sophisticated speculation, but a word of what God asks, of what God expects of us. Again it is a word calling for belief, for the response that will make us God-followers (as Abraham was, but even more, as disciples of Jesus Christ).

In interpreting Scripture, one must guard against the tendency to interpret oneself into the text. Our faith and our experience influence our interpretation.

We must come to the Scripture willing to have it speak to our presuppositions and correct them. The experience of Christ in my life, or in the covenant community, is necessary for proper interpretation of the Scripture, but I must also recognize that some dimensions of experience are also tainted and may be cause for errors in interpretation.

It is important that I allow the Scripture to speak for itself and let it achieve its purpose in me. "The aim of interpreting the New Testament texts," says Oscar Cullmann, "is to understand the faith of the first Christians, its origin, its content, and the manner in which it is fixed in the New Testament. . . . The ultimate goal of exegesis is fully attained only when this faith is subsquently achieved by us."[2] The dynamic aspect of interpretation is not in the concepts so much as in the expression of a transformed life. We are to live our understanding, to be *walking in the resurrection*.

The Word of God in Jesus of Nazareth did not end at the cross. The resurrection of Jesus Christ is the extension of this Word of God in all time. To hear God is to become a God-follower. To hear Him in Jesus Christ is to become a disciple who lives with the Master. This relationship is not to a way of life illustrated by Jesus of Nazareth several thousand years ago, but a friendship with Jesus Christ as a contemporary Person today who extends the meaning of His life into our own.

Knowing God is incomplete until we know Him in Jesus Christ. Knowing God is academic unless we respond to His call in faith. Jesus said, "Not every one who says to me, 'Lord, Lord,' shall enter the kingdom of heaven, but he who does the will of my Father who is in heaven" (Matthew 7:21). So Paul writes, "If then you have been raised with Christ, seek the things that are above, where Christ is, seated at the right hand of God. Set your minds on things that are above" (Colossians 3:1, 2).

Walking in the resurrection is living in faith in Christ. It is hearing and knowing God in His full Word in the risen Lord. This means sharing the continuing character and purpose of His life, hearing His call, living in His will. Our salvation and our discipleship is an experience of grace in which we are daily saying yes to the Lord. This is the gospel — that God has come to us with a calling that is clearly expressed in Jesus of Narareth and to which we can now respond. Knowing God is a matter of the will more than of the mind. To know Him is to know a faith that obeys; to respond is to let God be God in one's life. To walk in the resurrection is to walk with the Master. This obeying-faith is expressed in a prayer of Thomas á Kempis:

> O Lord, You know what is the better way; let this or that be done as You shall please. Give what You will, and how much You will, and when You will. Deal with me as You know, and best pleases You, and is most for Your honor. Set me where You will, and deal with me in all things as You will. I am in Your hand; turn me round and turn me back again, even as a wheel. Behold I am Your servant, prepared for all things, for I desire not to live to myself, but to You, and oh that I could do it worthily and perfectly.

UNDERSTANDING ONESELF

3

Understanding Oneself

From earliest childhood the quest for fulfillment begins to shape our lives. We dream of what we would like to be or do. But whatever our choice, happiness comes in finding fulfillment rather than in the status of the position we hold. This fulfillment comes through being at peace with oneself, one's God, one's associates, and with the world. But such fulfillment is illusive. Many people live most of their lives without this harmony, obsessed by the fear, the anxiety, that death will overtake them before they find meaning in life. This fear (called "finitude anxiety" by psychologists) becomes a whip that drives a person from one pursuit to another in his quest for meaning. Any attempt to understand oneself apart from the deepest level of meaning or fulfillment is superficial.

The individual is a part of humanity. One cannot adequately understand himself without understanding humanity or humanness. This raises a question as old as human thought, "What is man?" It leads to the question of the serpent in the Garden of Eden, "Yea, hath God said?" (Genesis 3:1, KJV). The implication of the serpent's question is, "Who are you? A dependent, circumscribed, limited person?" But people fail to see that their greater freedom is in saying "yes" to God, finding freedom in a fulfillment of their essential being.

We are not free when we profess not to need God, for then we are slaves to ourselves. When we live under the lordship of self we are very limited persons. We are free only when we stand under the lordship of Christ, under the One who opens the universe of meaning for our participation. Here, before Him, we can be honest, absolutely honest, with ourselves as an act of being honest with God.

But as a part of humanity, we must still ask, "What is man?" This question has goaded philosophers, prodded theologians, disturbed politicians, and hounded psychologists. We are told that man is a thinking animal, or a social and political being, or a moral being, or a being made in the image of God. This latter concept gives man his greatest dignity and elevates humanity to its highest sense of identity. It is on this concept that we must reflect.

What does it mean to say that man is a being created in the image of God? This Word of Scripture, the highest designation for mankind, gives the individual a basis for self-understanding. (See Genesis 1:20-27.) To be made in God's image—that is said of no other aspect of creation, of no flower, tree, or animal. Humans are the masterpiece of God's creation, an order of beings different from all living things, because they have been created in the image of God. Biologically, a human is much like an animal, but in his essential self he is different.

Man is made in God's image in that he is a person

with self-awareness, with the ability to think with self-transcendence; one who can reason, love, choose, assume responsibility for his decisions and activities, and fellowship with others in genuine interchange of thoughts and spirit. Man is not only a biological or social creature. He has a spiritual essence which is fulfilled only at the level of fellowship. Being made in God's image, complete fulfillment is achieved only when man experiences fellowship at the highest level — relationship with God.

Understanding ourselves is basic to our understanding of all else.[1] Our basic need of self-fulfillment cannot be met apart from self-understanding. To become a complete, secure person, we must know our limitations which need correction, as well as recognize our particular strengths and achievements. Honesty with ourselves will give us a degree of security and trust in ourselves. Honesty with God will bring us to the highest level of trust. It is unfortunate when we can have confidence in others, whom we know only in a limited way, and yet not achieve trust in ourselves. When we are honest we know where we have strengths that can be trusted and where those weaknesses are that cannot be trusted. The insecure person is usually guilty of not being honest with himself before God so that he can trust himself in God's grace and love. Likewise, to appropriate God's grace in specific areas of need we must thoroughly understand ourselves. These two dimensions belong together: (1) a well-integrated personality within oneself and (2) the integration of one's personality with God and man.[2]

The past several decades have seen the dawning of a new day in the Christian use of psychology to help us understand ourselves. Psychology, as a science, is not to be manipulated by Christian premises. However, as a science it is limited to the levels of gathering data, experimentation, and analysis. It tells us how things are, not how they ought to be. It is at the level of interpretation that one's world-view takes the findings of psychology and interprets their meanings for life. It is at this point that Christian faith, without violating science itself, brings its interpretation to bear upon life, utilizing all the benefits of science. In this way clinical psychology, professional counseling, and psychiatric therapy, administered with Christian love and faith, have been used of the Holy Spirit to bring healing of mind and emotions, of self-understanding and relationships with others. Group therapy, family therapy, and sensitivity therapy, when experienced in the context of redeeming love, have been effectively used by people of God for the discovery of new freedom and wholeness. But these exposures should always be experienced under the consciousness of the work of Christ to restore God's image in us.

Currently this quest for self-understanding is almost an obsession. But persons in this pursuit without Christ will fail to achieve fulfillment so long as they do not recognize the dimension God can bring to one's life. We cannot find fulfillment simply in navel gazing, although we may discover in this exercise our own dependence. Nor will we find fulfillment in the exercise of stripping our souls naked in the pursuit of some joyous climax of honesty. But wholeness, the fulfillment of becoming, is not found apart from the realization of God's image within us. This realization is a maturing in Christ, moving beyond spiritual adolescence in our way of relating to God. Rather than neurotic or psychopathic prayers we come to the Master with the denial of our own self-interests and become truly a partner with Him. Prayer becomes an act of faith, a life of walking in the Spirit.

Humanness has at least four dimensions: (1) the man-thought dimension, (2) the man-it dimension, (3) the man-man dimension, and (4) the man-God dimension. To understand oneself, one's quest for fulfillment, there must be harmony in the way one relates to all four of these dimensions, for man is basically a unit. The way we deal with one part of our life affects every other part. For example, worry, anxiety, and nervous tension affects the health of the body. Consequently, one must examine himself in depth to avoid interfering with God's harmony for the whole. A healthy life requires honest self-examination. But this is not done as an end in itself, or as a cure-all for isolated problems. It is rather a discipline of the self which finds fulfillment in the renewal of God's image within us. Negative analysis must always be followed by positive affirmation.

With this understanding of humanity we look further at the question, What is wrong with man? If man is made in the image of God is he not basically good? However, the answer regarding man's goodness must also include the evidence of man's evil. Both the evidence of life and the Scripture tell us that man is sinful. Our own experience tells us that we are sinful. In our quest for fulfillment we may try to deny the evil and promote the good, but sooner or later, usually sooner, we become fully convinced of a problem we can not expel. It is part of us. At the core of our being something is wrong. We have not only sinned, but we are sinful. Our very self must be called into judgment before the higher tribunal of our personality, and with thought and moral responsibility our honesty now takes on a new dimension.

What is this sinfulness that we cannot expel? Is it a power that stands against the good, forcing us to choose between good and evil? Or is it even more subtle, something that simply perverts the good to wrong ends? The more one reflects on the problem of sin, the more it appears to be the latter. Sin is the perversion of the good, of God's image in us.

Often sin is what we don't do! It is our failure to find fulfillment in fellowship with God, to know the highest level of spirit-fulfillment for which we were created. We fail most often, at least I do, in areas of the spirit — of being understanding, gracious, companionable, loving — and yet it is this level which is most important. Whatever our occupation in life, it is not of primary significance. More important is the person we bring to our calling, a whole person with sound spiritual, mental, and emotional health.

It is at this point that we find our answer in Jesus Christ, whose person expressed the greatest degree of humanness with love and acceptance. The Bible says, "God . . . through Christ reconciled us to himself" (2 Corinthians 5:18). The fact that God could come in human flesh is the greatest affirmation of humanness that the world has ever known! That God could become a man affirms the basic meaning and character of our existence — the truth that we are created in God's image. Further, the Incarnation affirms humanness and thereby shows us that sinfulness and humanness are not synonymous. This means that the new life in Christ, the fulfillment which He works in us, is a fulfillment of true humanness, a quality of life which we find exhibited in Jesus of Nazareth.

Paul's words in 2 Corinthians 5:17 — "If any one is in Christ, he is a new creation; the old has passed away, behold, the new has come" — find their character in the person of Jesus. The salvation which He brings is to restore our brokenness, correct our perversions, renew our relationship with God, and rebuild God's image! This is new, for it is not within us; it is of grace, for it could never be achieved by us. "For by grace you have been saved through faith" (Ephesians 2:9). *Walking in the resurrection* is living in this newness, this fulfillment in Christ.

But over against this answer in Christ stands man's basic problem of self-deification. The very quest for fulfillment has been perverted into a self-centeredness which closes the life against God. Rather than letting God be God in one's life we seek to be god for our own life. Self-deification is not expressed in its most subtle form by the moral perversions which are often the more obvious sins. Rather, it is expressed most subtly in the spirit of a person's life. The more subtle nature of our sinfulness is the sophisticated quest for the fulfillment of life apart from our turning to God. In this quest men may pursue culture, art, philanthropic programs, political or social roles, educational and scientific achievements as ends, as though they would bring fulfillment. If we recognize the truth of Christ, that fulfillment is in being rather than in doing, that it is realized in the renewal of God's image within us, then we can at the same time enjoy culture, art, benevolence, social and political relations, educational and scientific pursuits as an experience of sharing God's creative purposes for the service of our fellows. Education, culture, and art is for people's sake. In contrast to self-deification stands the towel and basin with which Jesus washed His disciples' feet. (See John 13:1-20.) Walking in the resurrection is to share His mission of service. For the disciple the desire to rule another is always wrong.

Man, created in God's image, was created in and for community. No person is complete of himself without the "other." Fellowship is not a luxury; it is the stuff out of which the true nature of the soul is formed. The person who deifies himself soon discovers that he is using and misusing other people; he is trying to possess and control them. As they back away to save their own selfhood from being exploited, the self-deifying person becomes more lonely and more determined to impress himself upon others. The excesses to which we go at times in our quest for power and our use of it, in our immodesty and vain ornamentation, in our development of in-group language to secure a clique in which to satisfy our personal hungers — all these are a commentary on our self-attitude, our failure to understand ourselves correctly. At times, in our so-called experience of community in our clubs or select groups, we buttress our own need of security at the expense of others. Let a non-in-group person appear and he or she is confronted with all the conversation and quotations of the latest discussion or book they have read. How cruel the members of an in-group can be protecting their own security. How refreshing when a little genuine love seeps through and a person feels that he is accepted for who he is rather than for who he knows or what he has done. It is fellowship which is important in community, the development of the soul in its reflection of God's image, in its expression of love and its security of peace.

In the immortal words of John Donne, "No man is an island." None of us is complete without our interrelation with others. Once we act in faith, faith in Christ as Lord, we renounce our self-deification. We become aware of the wonderful way in which God has made us to belong together, to be a new people, a brotherhood in freedom and joy. In this new faith we also discover our own responsibility to be a true self, sharing something of worth with others. We begin caring for our brother, seeking to be an influence for good in his life. In the same way we seek the enrichment of our own life in grace and knowledge, in creativity and wisdom for the enrichment of the noble humanity of which we are a part.

Each succeeding generation stands in a meaningful history, for it is a history in which God is at work within humanity. No one can be a leech in society, a parasite, without sinning against humanity and its greater fulfillment. The indifferent and slothful are as guilty as the powermongers who in their self-deification exploit the created order and others for their own self-deception. The human mind is doubtless more skilled at rationalization than at any other act. Rationalization helps us keep our mental balance when things happen beyond our control that affect us deeply. At the same time, it is one of the more dangerous exercises of the mind. How easy it is to justify ourselves. To engage in depreciating ourselves is an equal deception, for we are punishing ourselves as a self-inflicted atonement for our sense of insecurity. Even in our confessions, or in our exercises of therapy, we decide how to handle the details that have made up our lives.

If we are to find wholeness, the healing of minds and spirits which have suffered from the brokennes of sin, we must be completely honest with ourselves. This means we must face our higher self honestly, God's image within us, and with a similar honesty face our perverted self. This is best done by facing Jesus Christ honestly — the one truly real or genuine Person the world has ever seen. In Him we can see the true picture of the image of God we are intended to be, and in contrast we can see and deal with our sinfulness or perversions.

When we are converted to Christ we change direction, we commit our lives to a new Lord, but we do not make our confession once-for-all. This is something that is always happening in the life of faith. We do not come to Jesus of Nazareth for salvation and then ignor Him. We come to Jesus to relate to Him. I need Jesus today to save me from the perverted person I would be today without Him. This is walking in the resurrection. To believe is to identify with Him. This identification involves the best understanding of ourselves possible, psychologically, intellectually, emotionally, and volitionally—sharing our life fully with the living Christ. In my own quest for the fullness of Christ I have been blessed with the prayer of St. Anselm of the twelfth century:

O Lord;
Let me seek You in longing,
And long for You in seeking;
Let me find You in loving,
And love You in finding.

EXPERIENCING RECONCILIATION

4

Experiencing Reconciliation

Reconciliation assumes a change in relationships. Once we were estranged; now we are sharing. Once we were in the grip of the spirit of rebellion; now we accept God's will for us and identify with Him. Once we were isolated by our self-interests; now we enjoy fellowship with others. Reconciliation affects the very essence of our personalities; it is not simply dealing with the wrongs we have done.

Reconciliation focuses on the persons involved. It is an affirmation of our worth in relationship with others. It is experienced when we refuse to concentrate exclusively on the issue and affirm the greater worth of the person. This is true between us and God, for God cares more about us than about what we have done! God acted in Christ to reconcile us, to show us how much He loves us. Even in the face of our rejection of Him at the deepest level of our being, He still reaches out to accept us. Of this, Paul writes, "We were reconciled to God by the death of his Son" (Romans 5:10).

But reconciliation involves both parties. We must recognize that fellowship with God is more important for us than any "advantage" of the sin which separates us from God. In reaching out for reconciliation we can share life with the Lord rather than continue the self-deification which stands against Him. Obviously the cost is on God's side. He forgives and accepts us — when we are the ones who have lived in rebellion. But reconciliation involves us as participants, for we must heed the call of grace and renounce our rebellion. We must respond to God in faith. We must open our lives to His fellowship.

In the Reformation of the sixteenth-century Protestants emphasized God's grace, justification by faith, the universal priesthood of believers, and the sanctity of all of life. Of these, justification by faith has often been seen as the most crucial. Now, looking back, some leading twentieth-century Protestant theologians suggest that the most basic principle of Protestantism is the universal priesthood of believers. This concept emphasizes the personal relationship of each individual to God through Christ. It stresses the worth of each person who can stand before God in full self-awareness and responsibility. We should also keep in mind another wing of the sixteenth-century Reformation described as the Radical Reformation, also known as the Anabaptist movement. For them justification by faith meant justification in relationship, not in a rite of confessional affirmation. Their concept of faith included a strong emphasis on the importance of fellowship and faithfulness.

The priesthood of believers was possible because of their fellowship with Christ. This movement developed a deep awareness of community. Young and old, women and men, participated together in the life of faith, in the bonds of brotherhood, and in the witness of Jesus Christ. They insisted on the necessity of being reconciled to God now in Jesus Christ, of sharing a new life of fellowship with Him and with His followers. This understanding of reconciliation was of utmost importance to them and brought to justification and sanctification the perspective of relationship with God.

In Protestantism the emphasis on justification has always seemed to eclipse sanctification in Christian doctrine. Similarly, the emphasis on the cross and the Passion of Christ has often stopped short of the resurrection and the new life in Christ confirmed by the presence of the Holy Spirit. But God has used some voices in every period to call us to the awareness of a more demanding faith. One may cite the Waldensians of the Middle Ages, the Hussites of the fifteenth century, the Anabaptists of the sixteenth century, the rise of German Pietism in the seventeenth century, the spiritual awakening under Wesley in the eighteenth century, and the revival movements of the nineteenth century as examples. But one must immediately add that each was more an emphasis than a new theology. Similarly, the twentieth-century experience of sharing in the work of the Holy Spirit is potentially such a renewal.

At the University of Basel, Markus Barth related a comment made to Billy Graham nearly two decades ago by his father, Karl Barth. He predicted that the 1970s would be characterized by theological attention being given to the Holy Spirit. Markus himself, commenting in recent lectures on Ephesians, on the cleansing of the church by washing and making it holy by the Word (5:25-27) stresses the importance of the church becoming holy rather than placing so much emphasis on the sacraments.

Paul gave us the key to this transformed life: "He who through faith is righteous shall live" (Romans 1:17). When Martin Luther read this verse it hit him so forcefully that he added the word "alone," *i.e.*, by faith alone. Too often in following this emphasis the matter of being righteous is lost in promoting the idea of "faith alone." We need to read, "He who through faith is righteous," with the understanding that we are to be righteous and that the way to experience this is by faith rather than legalism. Legalism, or trust in the law, can take us no further than the law, but faith in Christ takes us all the way to God. (See Philippians 3:9.)

Reconciliation, the experience of relationship with God in Christ, affects every aspect of our lives. Faith is not a concept that we hold; it is a fellowship in which we live. To fellowship with God means that He has accepted me, and forgiven me. This in itself is a totally transforming realization. To be forgiven means that the sinless God of the universe has released me from the dreadful consequences of my sin. He has absolved His own indignation by love and has let me go free. To understand that I am forgiven in love is enough to bring me into fellowship with Him. When we experience this love and forgiveness we will repudiate the sin that has estranged us.

To be reconciled to God, or restored in relationship with Him, is to be made wholly His. It then follows that sanctification (belonging completely to God) and justification (being completely accepted by God) are companion aspects of reconciliation. We are reconciled through Christ by His death, yet Paul adds, "We shall be saved by his life" (Romans 5:10, KJV). The new life of our salvation is ours in fellowship with the risen Christ. This is *walking in the resurrection*! Faith is never a "solid state." It is a relationship of response to the sovereignty of the gospel, the good news of God's promise of life in Christ and His faithfulness to His promise.

This discussion is not simply a theological or academic exercise, for this understanding has major practical implications. It introduces us to a whole new way of life. In his writings, Paul recognizes this perspective approximately 265 times by using the words "in Christ." This phrase refers to a present reality. When we talk of being "in love" we understand this to be a present relationship. When we speak of living "in matrimony" or "in celibacy," we are referring to a present state. So it is that living "in Christ" is a present relationship, a sharing of one's life with the Lord. It is not just a matter of what we get from the Lord — His forgiveness, His salvation, His answers to our prayers of need — but rather a matter of walking with Him. This relationship enables us to live differently than we did — with our former self-interests.

Christian discipleship is grounded in the experience of reconciliation. To claim to follow Christ apart from reconciliation is a direct repudiation of Jesus Christ as Savior and Lord.[1] Such an attempt is a new legalism, a work of the flesh, an effort to copy the Jesus-life, thereby making Jesus another law.

But discipleship is fellowship with Christ, a fellowship of the reconciled, a participation with the One who invited us to yoke ourselves with Him, "For my yoke is easy, and my burden is light" (Matthew 11:30). As Professor Gollwitzer has said, God's grace and human work does not stand in conflict. We are passive in receiving His grace but His grace makes us active — it does not allow us to be passive. God works in the world in and through the work of men. He calls men to cooperate with Him in His work.[2] The truly reconciled are disciples who share the work of Christ in the world. Our deeds of faith are also expressions of our prayers.

For those whose emphasis on justification by faith is not conditioned by this understanding of reconciliation, an emphasis on discipleship may appear to be an emphasis on works. But when we understand the meaning of reconciliation we see discipleship as living in grace, living in God's acceptance. When we are reconciled in Christ we are identifying with Him. This is the meaning of Jesus' words, "If you continue in my word, you are truly my disciples" (John 8:31). The Protestant church has too often excused itself from responsibility for discipleship, calling it "works righteousness." With this perspective many well-meaning Christians have dismissed their responsibility for a Christian lifestyle as it relates to economic, social, political, and personal issues. As disciples we belong first and always to Jesus Christ. Our primary citizenship is in the kingdom of heaven. Our lifestyle is guided by our Lord.

But this understanding of reconciliation is a threat

to the person who has wrapped his life around himself. This experience shatters the fortress of self-rule, and opens the door to a new Lord. Now all of our interests, thoughts, ambitions, affections, deeds, and relationships include Him. Now I not only admit to myself the needs of my inner self for therapy, but I open myself to a Lord who understands not only what I confess but the deepest levels of my motivation and self-deification. In this relationship He heals by restoring me to genuine selfhood. Paul wrote, "I have been crucified with Christ; it is no longer I who live, but Christ who lives in me; and the life I now live in the flesh I live by faith in the Son of God, who loved me and gave himself for me" (Galatians 2:20). As Paul Tournier has said, the ego has usurped the central place in our lives and forced the real self to the periphery, but the real self is restored with Christ at the center of life.[3] In reconciliation with Christ we experience the restoration of God's image within us: we become whole, genuine persons again.

This relationship lays us brutally bare before God. We stand naked of soul with our inner being open to God. But we are transparent before a Lord who loves us, who accepts us while He ministers healing. Similarly, we are to love others and share with them in prayer for the healing of relationships. Healing does not come in isolation within ourselves; it is given in relation with others. When we are reconciled to God we are reconciled to other people. To belong to God is to belong also to His people.

The evidence that we have been set free from the

isolation of self-deification is in our genuine fellowship with those about us. This sense of fellowship determines the character of the church or congregation, for the church is a fellowship of reconciled people, not simply a gathering of individuals for ritualistic exercises of confession. Such a fellowship becomes a brotherhood participating in the life of Christ together.

Persons reconciled to Christ share the meaning and purpose of Christ. Our relations with others are always conditioned to enhance the cause of Christ. Among the fellowship of the reconciled this means participation in worship, in encouragement, in the joys and pains of life, in the giving and receiving of counsel and rebuke, in discerning together the will of the Spirit, and in interpretation of the character of Christian discipleship. As we move among the nonreconciled, we become agents of reconciliation, expressing the love of Christ. We discern and expose the idolatries of secularism, we minister healing to the suffering, and we stand by our neighbor in prayer. This is what it means to participate in the priesthood of believers. To witness to the resurrection of Christ as one who is reconciled to Him is to introduce a radically different dimension into the life and thought of the neighbor. In so doing we become an agent of reconciliation in his life.

The resurrection of Jesus Christ is the breaking through of the "other world" into this one. The disciples on the Emmaus Road were participants in fellowship with One who brought both realms together in Himself. To be reconciled to Christ is to be a participant in eternal life now. When we experience this we are bound together in a covenant with Him. His person and His purpose now become our direction and our goal. We are reconciled, all rebellion against His will is repudiated, and we affirm His will for the total life.

There is no part of our commonlife which should not reflect this covenant relation with Christ. To be reconciled, to identify with the risen Christ, is a far higher level of Christian experience than that on which we so often live. Too often we seek only release from guilt and renewal of our peace. Actually, being reconciled to Christ may, in fact, disturb our "peace," while communicating the deeper peace of sharing His mission. Now we share a comradeship with Him that issues in the higher levels of relationship—love, reverence, and oneness.

One's Christian understanding is not complete if it fails to recognize the meaning of reconciliation through the risen Christ. Paul writes of this relationship, "For you have died, and your life is hid with Christ in God" (Colossians 3:3). It is as I share this relationship with Christ that I am free to live a new life. The old pattern of self-deification is now past, in a break as definite as death. A new life has begun, one born by union with Christ. From here on the meaning of life is found only in Him. This is now my identification, "If you confess with your lips that Jesus is Lord and believe in your heart that he is a living Lord whom you will serve, you shall be saved" (literal meaning, Romans 10:9). The saved life is the life reconciled to Christ, the life identified with Him. We are now at rest in His grace, His gracious acceptance, and we have serenity and peace while active in His mission. This is a life of *walking in the resurrection*.

A NEW CREATION in CHRIST

5
A New Creation in Christ

Christianity is a relational rather than a moralistic faith. We are not reconciled to a law but to a Person. The change in our lives is a relational change, for we are now in right relation to God. Paul writes, "For Christ is the end of the law for righteousness to everyone that believeth" (Romans 10:4, KJV). We now come to Christ for right relation with God, no longer to the law. Paul (in Philippians 3:9) also emphasized that we now have a righteousness through faith in Christ, not a righteousness of our own based on law. We stand before God as reconciled in Christ, not seeking to win access to Him through the law. But neither do we ignore His laws. Rather, we find them transformed by love from legal constraint into opportunities for filial obedience.

But to affirm a change in our lives that is relational is to affirm that we are changed. "If any one is in Christ, he is a new creation" (2 Corinthians 5:17). This newness is a change which affects our total person. It begins the moment we are reconciled in Christ. Jesus expressed it to Nicodemus as a "new birth," a second beginning of one's life. He told Nicodemus that we must have a spiritual birth. (See John 3:3-7.) This new beginning happens at the moment of our reconciliation. We are different because we have a new relationship to God through Christ.

It is only as I know Jesus as Lord that I am free from the tyranny of myself. To be free is to live under the right influence, with the right orientation. Freedom does not mean to have no Lord; freedom means to have a Lord who always pronounces us free. This does not mean that my life is limited. Rather, it is expanded to take in all that the Lord has for me to share. It is as though one said to the fish in the sea, "There it is. The water is all yours. Enjoy it." Or to the bird in the air, "There, the air is all yours. Enjoy it." So Christ says, "I give you the abundant life, enjoy it." (See John 10:10.) It was some time after my conversion before I understood this. Even as a Christian I lived by the "laws" of Christ, under constraint, rather than in the freedom of the life He offers. In fact, I tend to impose constraints on myself from my understanding of the will of Christ rather than being relaxed in the freedom of His love and life. To be free is to relate openly to Him. [1]

A change in relation also involves a change within us. When we know Jesus as Lord we also experience a change at the core of life. The center of control passes from oneself to Christ. There is a new love, a new fidelity. No longer is one wrapped up in self-interests. Rather, one shares the life of Christ. How easy this is to say — but how difficult to maintain as a conscious identification! Until one discovers the meaning of His presence, this identification is a self-imposed consciousness. But with the sense of His acceptance one can rest in His love with a sense of belonging. As in human love, personalities that relate closely affect one another. Christ shares with us in total understanding of our personality while we share in understanding and identifying with His Person. Inevitably our lives change and begin to reflect the image of Christ.

This change in us is spoken of in Colossians 3 as "putting off the old nature" and "putting on the new nature." We are not passive in this change, but are active participants in identification with Christ. As we read the Scripture we must say, "This is me. This has happened to me. This is happening to me." Paul means in this passage that we no longer allow sin to dominate our life but we identify with Christ. We now allow the Spirit of Christ to dominate our lives. We voluntarily place ourselves under the control of Christ. We cannot conjure up a new life in our own strength, but change takes place in us by the grace of Christ.

Romans 6 points out that in our baptism we identify with Christ's death (being buried with Him) and with His resurrection (walking in newness of life). Identifying with Christ, we consider ourselves dead to the old sinful self and alive to God in Christ Jesus. (See Romans 6:4, 6, 11.) This resurrection in our own lives awakens us to a new realm of association with Christ as different from our old existence apart from God as life is different from death.

The new life is given to us, but it is for us to explore and assimilate its potential. This is what is meant by "putting on the new nature." We put on a new life — a life of love, kindness, humility, meekness, patience, forgiveness, peace, thankfulness, joy, reverence, and obedience. (See Colossians 3:12-17.) We can claim these graces as our own as we share in the resurrection life. These graces contrast with our old feelings. Sometimes the old lifestyle tries to take over again, but we can claim our new nature in Christ. Each time the new dimension is experienced, the more real it becomes and the more distant are the inclinations to turn back to the old way of life. Any slip into the old patterns becomes more distasteful as we experience the new.

The life of wholeness is the resurrection life, sharing the freedom of Christ to live as new men. Should one allow himself to slip back into the old way? Obviously not. Shouldn't one identify fully, once and for all, with the new? Of course. But the nature of God's transforming grace is not automatic, nor is it impersonal in a way that would violate our personality or psychological structure. The identification with death to the old life and resurrection into the new is an identification of faith, not an impersonal fact of change. (See Romans 6:11.) Our holiness comes from our identification with Him, our belonging totally to Christ.

This belonging is no more static than love is in a happy marriage. We are relating to Christ, interacting with Him as we ponder His Word, pray, and fellowship with His people. If we fail to exercise ourselves in the graces of our new life we also soon fail to express the character of Christ. The great pianist Paderewski said that if he did not practice six hours in any single day he knew the difference, if he missed two days his friends knew the difference, and if he missed three days his audience knew the difference.

But there is more to this change. Sharing the resurrection life also involves sharing life in the Spirit. This is more than maximizing the spirit dimension of our own personalities. It is identifying with the Spirit of Christ. Jesus said it was to our advantage that He go away so that the Holy Spirit could come. He promised that He would send (or would baptize His disciples with) the Holy Spirit. (See John 16:7, 8; Acts 1:4, 5.) Paul wrote of the Holy Spirit being "poured out upon us richly through Jesus Christ our Savior" (Titus 3:6). And John writes that Christ "abides in us, by the Spirit which he has given us" (1 John 3:24). The presence of the Holy Spirit in our lives is another dimension of the change Christ works in us.

Christ, the One who baptizes with the Spirit, gives us the Holy Spirit when we confess Him as Lord. Baptism with the Spirit is another aspect of the privilege of reconciliation in Christ, just as is the new birth. But these two aspects are not synonymous. In the new birth our spirit is quickened or made alive in relation to God by the Spirit of Christ (Ephesians 2:1), while in the baptism with the Spirit we are given the Holy Spirit by Christ Himself to dwell in our lives. Now, as disciples, we are to walk in the Spirit (Galatians 5:21), to obey the Spirit (Acts 5:32), to be filled with the Spirit (Ephesians 5:18), and to honor the indwelling presence of the Spirit (Ephesians 4:30).

This mind-boggling reality, the indwelling presence of the Spirit, makes the new life dynamic and creative. The presence and power of the Spirit keep us free from the old self and create in us the character of the new life. His fruit in us makes us Christlike. His manifestations in us enrich the church. His life in us expresses the nature of Christ. (See Galatians 5:19, 20; 1 Corinthians 12 and 14; and John 16:8-14.)

This is the key to our sharing the resurrection life. Paul writes, "If the Spirit of him who raised Jesus from the dead dwells in you, he who raised Christ Jesus from the dead will give life to your mortal bodies also through his Spirit which dwells in you" (Romans 8:11). This is so fantastic that we can hardly grasp it. This power of the resurrection is a present reality, a newness of life brought to us by the Holy Spirit, that we may live in the will of Christ. This is the dynamic change that makes us new creatures. The life of the disciple, of the born-again person, of the reconciled one, is a life of new purpose, new principles, and above all a new partnership — with the Holy Spirit.

WALKING
in the
RESURRECTION

6

Walking in the Resurrection

The risen Christ expresses in His person the character of humanity that will make up His eternal order. John Calvin spoke of the ascension of Christ as His taking humanity to heaven as the guarantee that we can be there someday. The resurrection of Christ introduces a new humanity, a life beyond the power of death, beyond the limitations of the natural order, and free in the realm of the Spirit. The risen Lord expresses the meaning of love beyond the pain of suffering, of peace beyond the pleasures of life, and of fellowship in the Spirit beyond the securities of material things. Jesus calls us to share the quality of this new life now, as we see it in Him, for He already introduces us to the new order.

On February 24, 1527, the Swiss Brethren, or Anabaptists, as they were called, held a synod at Schleitheim near the Swiss-German border. This gathering of Christian disciples prayed and fellowshiped together until a great sense of the unity of the Spirit was impressed upon them. In the articles of faith which they adopted appears a unique phrase, rarely found in confessional statements. They spoke of those who desire "to walk in the resurrection of Jesus Christ."[1] This phrase is almost presumptuous, except that it appears in the context of an experience with Christ, of repentance, of forgiveness, of assurance of salvation, of identifying with Christ in His death and resurrection. The concept is grounded in Paul's words, "For if we have been united with him in a death like his, we shall certainly be united with him in a resurrection like his" (Romans 6:5; see also Colossians 3:1).

To share "in a resurrection like his" — what a fantastic calling, what a momentous relationship! This expression refers to the reality of a changed life, an expression of transforming grace. Paul expressed his great life-passion in the words, "That I may know him and the power of his resurrection" (Philippians 3:10). To live in the resurrection is to know in my life the power of the risen Christ, freedom from the death-dealing tendency to sin, fellowship that knows the openness of interchange with the Father, and fullness of life which has the quality of the eternal. Are these mere words, or is this not the very dynamic of identifying with Jesus as Lord, of being a member of His kingdom now, of being "partakers of the divine nature" (2 Peter 1:4)?

Walking in the resurrection is what Soren Kierkegaard called "contemporaneity" with Christ.[2] Not only does the resurrection mean that Jesus Christ is my contemporary, it means that I can associate with Him now, be involved personally with Him, and share contemporaneity with Him.

Just prior to His death on the cross, Jesus gave the disciples some of His most profound teaching regarding their future relationship with Him. (See John 14 to 17.) Jesus pointed the disciples beyond

His death to another relationship which they at that time did not understand, a relationship with a risen Jesus uniting them with the Father and the Holy Spirit. John 15 is a unique expression of what it means to abide in Christ, to live and walk in the resurrection.

Christ's resurrection took Him from the material world to the realm of the Spirit. Of this Jesus had said, "It is to your advantage that I go away, for if I do not go away, the Counselor will not come to you; but if I go, I will send him to you" (John 16:7). In going away Jesus helped free His followers from the tendency to localize God. He also introduced them to the spirit realm in a manner which was still personal and person-centered. The Father and the Spirit are both spoken of by Jesus as persons. Our relation to the spirit-realm is not impersonal but to a Father and the Spirit we have come to know in Jesus Christ.

In John 14:18-20 Jesus said, "I will not leave you desolate; I will come to you. Yet a little while, and the world will see me no more, but you will see me; because I live, you will live also. In that day you will know that I am in my Father, and you in me, and I in you." Jesus was speaking of His relation as risen Lord to His followers. To share with Him is to share a direct relationship with the Father, a fellowship of belonging and of purpose. Jesus said, "If a man loves me, he will keep my word, and my Father will love him, and we will come to him and make our home with him" (John 14:23). It is strange that people ask God for guidance when they will not obey His commands. The reconciled life is an obedient life, a life of love.

This unity with the Father has its classic expression in the prayer of our Lord in John 17. (See especially verses 16-23.) Here Jesus prays that His disciples may be one in the same way that He and the Father are one. This unity of Christians comes about by Christ being in us as freely as He is in the Father and the Father in Him. This is not a unity that can be structured or imposed by human organization; it is a unity that is given to us in grace. Only as we share the life of Christ, as we walk in the resurrection, do we know the unity given by Christ. And this gift of grace is always happening. Where people get together who are sharing the resurrection life, they experience the freedom and joy of His fellowship. The Emmaus Road experience happens again.

The key to this experience is found in Jesus' emphasis in John 15 on our abiding in Him. In the picture of the vine and the branches Jesus is teaching the resurrection life. "I am the vine." These words place the source of life in Christ. "You are the branches." These words express our dependence upon the vine for life. How is this abiding more than a mystical frame of mind? How is it an actual relationship? Jesus answers that it is by love and obedience. (See John 15:7-15.) By the power of love we experience the lordship of Christ. By obedience to His Word we express the lordship of Christ. To walk in the resurrection is to walk in relationship to the finished or complete expression of the will of God made known by Jesus. John tells us that one who says he is a Christian should live in the same way Jesus lived. (See 1 John 2:6.)

Such a relationship results in communion, for fellowship grows out of participation together. This is what prayer is all about — fellowship with God. The risen Christ, at God's right hand, is our representative with the Father before the hosts of heaven. He is our High Priest. In Him every believer exercises the priesthood of ministering before the Lord in praise and thanks, prayer and reverence. Jesus affirms in John 14:12 that the works of His followers will extend far beyond His own because He goes to the Father and opens the way for God's purpose to be extended to all. He introduces a new level of prayer, that we may ask anything consistent with His name and He will do it, that the Father may be glorified in the Son. (See John 14:13.) In John 15:16 He repeats this promise in relation to the fruit our lives will bear as we abide in Him. Again in John 16:23, 24, the promise is stated as a new level of prayer, opened by His death on the cross and His resurrection, with the key to effective prayer always tied to asking in harmony with His name.

There is no real prayer for the disciple other than post-resurrection prayer (prayer which is in relation to the risen Christ). And how do we pray in His name? Just as He demonstrated in His prayer in John 17. He prayed in the name of the Father, in harmony with that which would glorify the Father, no matter what it cost Himself. This is the deepest level of prayer.

Significantly, Jesus' greatest teaching on the Holy Spirit is in this same section of John's gospel. The experience of the Holy Spirit is directly related to our association with the risen Christ. Possibly one reason the knowledge of the Holy Spirit is so limited among many Christians is that they do not think in terms of relating to the risen Christ today. When we know the meaning of sharing with the risen Christ we are operating in the realm of the Spirit. Jesus said in John 14:16, 17 that in His going away the Holy Spirit would come to us. He promised to send the Holy Spirit from the Father, and that the Spirit would bear witness of Christ. (See John 15:26, 27.)

In chapter 16 He relates what the Holy Spirit will do in the life of the disciple. First, He will convict the world of sin by magnifying Christ in us, of righteousness by expressing right relation with God in our lives, and of judgment by demonstrating in our lives that Satan is already judged and defeated (verses 7-11). Second, the Spirit will enrich our lives as disciples by giving us insight into truth, by bringing to us confirmation of the Word of Christ, and by glorifying Christ in our lives (verses 12-15). This passage is a classic expression of the work of the Spirit in the life of the disciple.

To walk in the resurrection is to walk in the Spirit. Jesus, the only One who baptizes with the Spirit, gives His Spirit to us when we confess Him as Lord. The presence of the Spirit is the confirmation of Christ's lordship. As we are led of the Spirit, we are abiding in Christ. The disciple knows the reality of the indwelling Spirit and daily we open our lives to be filled with the Holy Spirit. We should acknowledge His presence each day, practicing the presence of the Spirit.

I am often away from home in meetings and I may be on the other side of the world from my wife, but I am never outside the awareness that I belong to Esther and Esther belongs to me! So it is with life in the Spirit. As disciples we are never outside the awareness that we belong to Him and that He belongs to us and with us. The Spirit-filled life is the life that is possessed, led, and controlled by the Spirit. On our part this means yieldedness and obedience. *Walking in the resurrection* is walking in the Spirit, expressing the fruit of the Spirit, serving in the power and with the gifts and enrichment of the Spirit.

A Christ-centered faith is incomplete apart from this dimension of relationship with the risen Christ. As contemporaries of Christ we can literally accept His words, "Lo, I am with you always, to the close of the age" (Matthew 28:20). When David Livingstone's wife died in Africa, he helped make the coffin, prepared her body for burial, read the words of faith at her funeral, and helped lower her body into the grave and cover it with earth. Then taking his New Testament he read, "Lo, I am with you always, to the close of the age," and turning to his faithful helpers he said, "Jesus Christ is too much of a gentleman not to keep His word, Let's get on with the task."

CITIZENS
of
CHRIST'S KINGDOM

7

Citizens of Christ's Kingdom

One of the most revolutionary convictions one can hold is to believe in the present, spiritual, universal kingdom of Christ and to give it loyalty above all else. To confess in all seriousness that Jesus is Lord, and that we belong to His kingdom now, puts us on a collision course with secularism. To affirm that the realities of the kingdom of Christ and His purposes take precedence over all material things and their use contradicts materialism, whether it be capitalism or Marxism. To believe that the kingdom of Christ is universal, or global, and that the disciple of Christ has a primary responsibility to all other followers of Christ around the globe supersedes all nationalism. But it is this reality of the kingdom of Christ, its universal and transcultural character, which calls people of all lands to become fellow disciples of the Master.

Michael Sattler wrote to the Reformer of Strasbourg, Martin Bucer, in October 1527, "The Christian's citizenship is in heaven, not on the earth. Christians are the family of God and citizens of the saints, not of the world."[1] This expression was a recognition that there are two kingdoms with which man has to do. One is the kingdom of heaven, in which Jesus is confessed as Lord, and in which persons by a voluntary confession of faith identify with Him as their King. The other kingdom is of this world, dominated by evil, big money, status, and power.

Jesus faced this choice when the prince of this world, Satan, offered to turn over to Him all the kingdoms of the world. Christ was loyal to the higher kingdom then and throughout His life. Just before His death Jesus said, "The ruler of this world is coming. He has no power over me" (John 14:30). Again Jesus said, "My kingdom is not of this world: if my kingdom were of this world, then would my servants fight, that I should not be delivered to the Jews: but now is my kingdom not from hence" (John 18:36, KJV). The closing book of the New Testament, Revelation, presents Jesus not only as the Lamb of God but as King of kings and Lord of lords. Jesus told us He will return to deal with the nations of this earth as a King over all. And Paul writes that Jesus will fulfill the building of His kingdom and will turn it over to the Father. (See 1 Corinthians 15:24.)

In the New Testament the kingdoms of God and of this world always stand in contrast, two separate reference points. In the Old Testament, Israel as God's people amidst the nations was the focus of contrast. God created Israel by His own call of grace and for His own purpose of having a channel through which to introduce Himself to the world in a variety of ways which culminated in the coming of Christ. (See Ezekiel 16:3.) But now that Christ has come, introducing the kingdom of God in a more complete way, the mystery that was hidden from the foundation of the world, as Paul refers to it in Ephesians 1, is now known, that persons of all nations are to make up the people of God. This is the kingdom Christ is building through the redemption of the cross and the resurrection.

The kingdom of Christ is a new humanity which He is creating in fellowship with Himself. Members of His kingdom are the spiritually transformed, those who walk in the resurrection. Paul writes of this transformation that God "has delivered us from the dominion of darkness and transferred us to the kingdom of his beloved son" (Colossians 1:13). It is this kingdom of which Jesus said, "My Father assigned to me a kingdom" (Luke 22:29). This is the reality which filled the message of Christ with something radically different from that of the religious leaders about Him. He introduced the kingdom of God, a new reality breaking into time and extending beyond time. The creation of a new people of God, who will be identified with God and live forever with Him, is the central purpose of His redeeming grace.

The meaning of the kingdom for our personal lives may be expressed as "the rule of God." This means for me that as I pray the "Disciple's Prayer," asking God that His will be done on earth as it is done in heaven (Matthew 6:10), I am willing the will of God for my life. In his significant teaching on prayer, Glen Clark quotes Henry Nelson Weiman: " 'The kingdom was Jesus' word for the toal maximum of possibility for good which can be accomplished in us, and through us, and round about us, inasmuch as we make right adaptation to God.' "[2] This definition personalizes my participation in the kingdom, and the perspective that my life is contributing to the spread of the kingdom.

Glen Clark says that he prayed constantly to "abide in the kingdom of heaven every moment of the day, and inspire others to abide there also.[3] This is the meaning of Jesus' words, "But seek first his kingdom and his righteousness, and all these things shall be yours as well" (Matthew 6:33). The disciple's commitment is to Christ, to put His kingdom first in whatever situation we find ourselves. We have enlisted in the cause of Christ. He is our Captain and we are committed to serve Him to the death — but even more, to live as His servants in the world. Wherever Jesus is ruling, there is the kingdom.

Earlier in this chapter reference was made to the Schleitheim Synod, led by Michael Sattler, a sixteenth-century Anabaptist. This devout man was burned for his faith in Christ on May 10, 1527. Sattler and many of his Anabaptist associates believed in the reality of the kingdom of God. They considered their lives expendable for the cause of this kingdom. Among letters written from prison cells across Europe in the sixteenth century (where literally thousands were executed for their faith) are numerous references to the reality of the kingdom to which they belonged and were about to enter fully through martyrdom.[4] They were so certain of the lordship of the risen Christ and of His kingdom that this reality became a greater factor in their consciousness than the pain of suffering. Their songs and witness in the hour of death is evidence that they were *walking in the resurrection*.

This kingdom does not come by human organization. Jesus said, "The kingdom of God cometh not with observation" (Luke 17:20, KJV). Although He said to the scribes and Pharisees, "The kingdom of God is in the midst of you" (Luke 17:21), yet for the most part they failed to recognize it. Many of His parables teach us how the kingdom lays its claims upon the minds and hearts of men, and how they follow in the Spirit of God. Of the nature of the kingdom, Paul writes, "For the kingdom of God is not food and drink but righteousness and peace and joy in the Holy Spirit" (Romans 14:1). The disciple, walking in the Spirit, lives now as a participant in the kingdom of God.

The conviction of the Christian church regarding the ultimate destiny of mankind and the world is severed from its roots if it speaks only of a future happening in Christ's return. It must also see the faith as grounded in the resurrection and being currently expressed in the building of the kingdom moving toward its fuller expression. Too often we debate our millennial views and underemphasize the lordship of the risen Christ who builds the kingdom. From Augustine to the present, the church has had a prominent amillennial emphasis identifying the reign of Christ with His rule in the church. Alongside this has existed a strong premillennialism, emphasizing the coming millennium when Jesus will reign on earth in a manner affecting all people and nations. I agree that the New Testament teaches a great coming culmination for the kingdom of Christ. However, we dare not fail to emphasize the reality of the kingdom of Christ now as He invites men and women to Himself around the world, building a kingdom of those who call Him Lord.

God's plan is oriented toward the proclamation of the gospel to the whole world. He opens the way for all persons, regardless of their religious background or world-view, to come to Christ. His kingdom is made up of persons "from every tribe and tongue and people and nation" (Revelation 5:9). The channel through which God expressed this saving work in history was the Jewish community. And God, in His overarching plan, is not through with the Jew. Referring to Romans 9 to 11, Professor Cullmann says, "From this passage, we understand that even today the Jews remain the elect people, and that they have a permanent role to play in salvation history. According to Paul, God made use of their unbelief in order to include the Gentiles in salvation history. The Gentiles were grafted onto the Jewish tree, but the foundation is still this Jewish tree, and at the end even Israel according to the flesh will be saved."[5] This goal adds dimension to our purpose of sharing the present meaning of the kingdom of God.

Present-day Israel needs to be seen in context with God's universal purpose for all people. The Gentile has been grafted into the historic Judaic roots. The Arab is my brother. The Middle East conflict calls me to recognize God's work among the Arabs even while He uses the Jews as a reminder of a special revelation of Jehovah. He may even be working out one great Semitic federation for the whole Middle East! (See Isaiah 19.) But whatever the future details of His plan, we know His purpose — the building of a kingdom open to all.

The kingdom of God centers in Jesus Christ, and is expressed today in His body, the church. But this is not the institutional form of the church. Rather, it is the new people of God which He is creating.

This people is global, transnational, a fellowship of the redeemed who know the new life in Christ. This dynamic fellowship replaces the old organizational Israel as God's channel of confrontation. George Eldon Ladd, who has written effectively on this issue, says, "No longer is the kingdom of God active in the world through Israel; it works rather through the church." [6]

If the kingdom is not a structure, "but righteousness and peace and joy in the Holy Ghost," what does this mean for the life of the disciple? When we share the lordship of Christ and walk in the reality of the resurrection, we recognize that kingdom membership affects the way we live. While walking in the resurrection is more than following an outline of ethical behavior, it certainly does call for living a life of love.

But the approach to ethics for the disciple is not primarily philosophical. The disciple's ethic is basically centered on Christ. Jesus Himself is the norm for this ethic. As risen Lord He extends the meaning of the life He lived on earth into all time and into all cultures. God has acted in the saving event in Christ. First we are accepted in Christ, and then it becomes ethically clear what we ought to become in Him (See Colossians 3:1-3.)

Accepting reconciliation through Christ as basic in Christian experience, we can relate ethics to Christ in the same way that we relate salvation to Christ. Reconciled to Him, Jesus is our Lord. In this relationship His will is now our will. His Person is the norm for our understanding of the good and complete life. We accept the whole Jesus — what He said, as a revelation of God's will; what He did, as a fulfillment of God's will; and what He was, as an expression of God's will. What He said becomes a guide for the disciple to follow, but also the way He lived and expressed Himself in love, forgiveness, and service is likewise a guide for us.

In Colossians 3, Paul follows his reference to our sharing resurrection newness with specific ethical instructions. When we truly believe in Christ as Lord, our belief in His lordship will affect the way we live. By obeying the will of Christ we express the genuineness of our reconciliation in a way other than a mere moralism. This is an ethic of the new life, an ethic of personalism, an expression of the restoration of God's image within us.

Because the disciple's conduct is related directly to Christ, we must recognize ethics as central in the experience of faith. A reconciling faith involves fidelity or faithfulness. We can say, "The just shall live his faith!" To know Christ as Lord means the transformation of one's total way of life. As members of the kingdom of Christ, our style of living corresponds to the character of His kingdom. The question for us is always, What does it mean to follow Christ as a disciple? By this I do not mean that we follow a checklist of Jesus' teachings, but rather that we share with Christ as a living, present reality.

Discipleship is kept from legalism by sharing the resurrection life, by living under the direction of the Spirit. As we walk in the Spirit we will live in love, holiness of life, freedom amidst material things, and service to our fellowman. Our sense of responsibility for social concerns will be directly related to our commitment to Christ and His love. He calls us both to love God and to love our fellowman. These are the basic commandments Christ lays on His disciples.

To belong to the kingdom of Christ is to be in the world, but not of it. It is to live in the will of God among our fellowmen. We are called to share the power or quality of the resurrection in life. This relationship to Christ frees us as disciples in the world. It is spoken of by Jesus in His prayer before death, "I do not pray that thou shouldst take them out of the world, but that thou shouldst keep them from the evil one. They are not of the world, even as I am not of the world" (John 17:15, 16). Therefore, as kingdom members, we need to discern how Jesus was "not of the world" while in it, as our guide in discerning how we can be in the world and not of it. The disciple, in understanding himself, must keep check on whether his decisions and actions are motivated by the spirit of this age or by the Spirit of Christ. Actually, this is the way of freedom -- to be liberated from the pressure to conform to society, to refuse to live in affluence at the expense of others, to serve rather than to manipulate others or do violence to their spirit.

The disciple is called to live a new life in society, not to try to create a new society for the world. In whatever degree society is changed for the good, it is enhanced by the influence of persons who experience a change in their own lives by His resurrection power. One cannot fully experience the new birth (the new life) without discovering what it means to love all people, to do violence to no one, and to live modestly in the midst of a status-seeking humanity. The new life calls us to show love for our neighbor. Today as never before we must find ways to minister to the needy, to share the world's resources with the malnourished, and to bring deliverance to the suffering.

Jesus taught the character of the kingdom as a spiritual force, a personal identification of disciples scattered through the world, which by the quality of the new life is an influence for God among others. This is expressed in a whole series of parables, especially in Matthew 13. The parable of the wheat and the tares makes this clear, emphasizing that Christ's kingdom will not come as a structure which dominates society, but the wheat and tares will grow together in the world until His judgment at the end of this age.

That this kingdom of Christ is global, and that all nations will be judged for the way they have acted in relation to God's work in history through Israel, is clearly expressed in Matthew 25:31-46. It is important to note in this account that the judgment for the failure of men to act in obedience to the King of kings is given in terms of the kind of service or ministry which meets the personal needs of their fellowman. In other words, the character of the kingdom now in society is the expression of the new life in Christ which lives in love toward others. In this same vein, we have quoted Jesus, "Not every one who says to me, 'Lord, Lord,' shall enter the kingdom of heaven, but he who does the will of my Father who is in heaven" (Matthew 7:21).

My faith is not authentic if I only want to enjoy the experiences of piety but will not soil my hands in loving service to my fellowman. If I believe in the Trinity, the ultimate expression of mutuality of love, I will extend this love to other personalities.

To be a member of the kingdom of Christ is a present reality, my identification today. My citizenship as a disciple is in heaven and I take my direction from there. In the world I am an ambassador for my King, a representative of my Sovereign in an alien land. (See 2 Corinthians 5:20.) This life is a pilgrimage, but one for which the way is known, the destiny sure. Our identification is clearly with the King of kings in contrast to secularism which can only affirm belief in man but not in God.

Professor Jan Milü Lockman, of the University of Basel and formerly from Czechoslovakia, tells of receiving from the United States a copy of *Time* magazine with a cover article entitled "God Is Dead." At the same time he received another magazine from a communist country with the cover article entitled "God Isn't Quite Dead!" Secularism is simply another form of atheism. It orients life around man as though God did not exist. To confess Christ as Lord and affirm the reality of His kingdom is revolutionary. But this is our stance as disciples — a stance in which we are on the offensive, confronting the world in all its power with One whose risen life and resurrection power is the ultimate reference in this world.

I have stood among the colossal ruins of Roman and Greek culture at Baalbeck, Athens, Ephesus, and a dozen other sites, and it seemed I could hear again the words of those early Christians, "Jesus is Lord, not Caesar." The majestic ruins testify to the grandeur of civilizations of the past, but the words of the gospel, the power of Paul's message written from the prison cells of the Roman Empire, live on, transforming lives and building a kingdom by introducing men to the King of kings.

The CHURCH as a COMMUNITY

8

The Church as a Community

The church is a fellowship, not an institution. In the Luther Bible the New Testament word for church, *ecclesia*, is translated *Gemeinde*. This church, which Christ is building, is a new people of God, a people who share a new life as disciples of Christ, a people who walk in the resurrection! This people have in common their commitment to Christ and the experience of the transformation of life wrought in them by the Holy Spirit. This means that the church is a community (*Gemeinschaft*) of the redeemed.

I use the word "community" to keep us from almost automatically thinking of the church as an institution or ogranization. The church is a fellowship of people who have experienced conversion or regeneration by the Holy Spirit and who function responsibly as disciples of Jesus Christ, together sharing love and discipline, hearing and interpreting the Word, and witnessing corporately and individually for Jesus as Lord.

As I have known and shared the Christian life for over a quarter of a century, three aspects of the Christian life have become increasingly important to me. *The first is the authority of Scripture*, the Word of God written, the one sure guide for faith and life. As a disciple, I must come to the Word of Christ with my mind already made up to obey Him. *The second is the guidance of the indwelling Holy Spirit.* As great as were the experiences of my early awareness of receiving the Holy Spirit, the reality of His indwelling presence equipping me to serve Christ in each occasion of life has become even more crucial. *And the third is the subject of this chapter, the importance of Christian community.* There is no substitute for the fellowship of believers, a brotherhood of disciples who despite their differences identify with Christ as Lord and commit themselves to follow His example and teachings. [1]

Brotherhood is a happening. It is not structured nor is it assumed to be the character of the organized church. Rather, brotherhood is the sharing of mutual love in the fellowship of disciples as an expression of the love of Christ which has called us each into this *Gemeinschaft.* The believer's covenant with Christ is at the same time a covenant with the people of Christ. This is the nature of Christian community, sharing with the new people of God as a primary frame of reference. Here is where we belong; these are our people.

As citizens of the kingdom of heaven we identify with what the Apostle Paul calls a colony of heaven on earth. (See Philippians 3:20.) He uses the metaphor of the Roman colony, an outpost in an alien territory, to describe the church. This is not to imply that the church is not a part of this world's life. Rather, the church is an expression in the world of a new humanity, a people reconciled to God, a people in whom the restoration of God's image keeps coming through as a transparent quality. In fact, it is in our mutual love, in our giving and receiving counsel, in our sharing the material things with the needy, in our common worship together, and in our witnessing to the lordship of Christ — that we express what it means to be "in the world but not of the world."

But how do we experience brotherhood, a fellowship which is more than organization? We do not operate without organization, nor do we function as a corporate body without some structure. The church, as it is known in Christian history, has creeds that it confesses and rites which it performs. The experience of fellowship does not exclude these, but it is more. A gathered body may recite the Apostles' Creed together and yet miss the fellowship which this common experience should make natural. For the congregation to be a community of faith, a fellowship at the deepest level, there must be a common sharing of the covenant of love in the Spirit of Christ. In this covenant relationship we become one people expressing our reconciliation to God and to each other, sharing in the quality of a new life, demonstrating that we are men and women made new by the Spirit of God.

Our Western individualism is a hindrance to genuine fellowship, for we tend to insulate ourselves from others. Each of us is inclined to limit our sharing to superficial exchanges rather than operating in a deeper covenant relation. To overcome our individualism we need to experience a deeper level of trust. We do not lay open our inner selves with persons we do not trust deeply. There is always the fear that our sharing may be misused. To open oneself to another person is to become vulnerable. But where there is assurance of mutual commitment to Christ, and awareness that each shares His resurrection life, we share a covenant of love which makes possible the deepest level of trust.

However, fellowship is more than sharing happenings in our lives. It is sharing the aspirations of the soul, the vision and dreams of what we seek to attain in Christ; it is exhorting and encouraging one another in faith. It is partnership in prayer at the deeper level of communing with one another as we commune with God. A hindrance to this level of fellowship is the moralism or legalism which accompanies all tendencies toward perfectionism. Often we are guilty of putting on a mask to impress people that we are a certain type of person when we know we are not!

Two masks cannot have fellowship. We cannot encourage another brother or sister in Christ unless we talk with the real person. And another individual cannot help us so long as the mask he addresses is not the real person we are deep down inside. Fellowship is dependent upon honesty, a transparency of the soul.

The church is the one place in society where the conditions for fellowship should be fully met. What a tragedy when lonely, isolated souls come to worship only to remain lonely, isolated souls in the crowd. The New Testament church is not a place where lonely souls come to partake of the sacrament or participate in religious liturgy without sharing the faith in covenant with others who are experiencing Christ. From the birth of the church the believers related so genuinely with each other that it affected their total lifestyle. (See Acts 2:43-47; 4:32-37.) Nothing, not even property, stood above or outside their covenant of love. Every issue of life was open to the brotherhood; the cause of discipleship had priority. Tithing is an expression of our covenant to relate material things totally to this covenant group.

In turn, the total church is enriched by sharing at this deeper level. In 1 Corinthians 12, 13, and 14, Paul discusses the gifts of the Spirit, and the way in which the Holy Spirit is always ready to give a particular congregation the gifts which it needs for its enrichment. These gifts may vary at different times to meet the needs which He sees, but He will give His gifts to the church as we desire His best for us.

One test of fellowship is whether we are prepared to recognize and utilize the gifts present in the fellowship of believers. Gifts of wisdom, management, and faith are often overlooked for the more spectacular gifts of oratory or healing. In Acts 6:1-7 internal needs developed that could easily have turned the early church from its primary mission, but the apostles instructed the believers to seek out men with gifts of management, who were full of the Holy Spirit and faith, to care for the physical needs of those who were being neglected. This permitted the apostles to continue their ministry of sharing the gospel. The fellowship of the new humanity which Christ is creating must responsibly and humbly recognize and employ the gifts provided by the Spirit of Christ. It is in respecting each other's gifts that we can "outdo one another in showing honor" (Romans 12:10). God's cure for jealousy is in calling us to respect His right to assign our brother his role in life. Mutual respect and participation is the character of covenant community.

Such a fellowship of Christians becomes a visible expression in society of the new people which God creates. This kind of church becomes an exhibit before the world of the resurrection power of Christ. We who know Christ as Lord are "a chosen race, a royal priesthood, a holy nation, God's own people" (1 Peter 2:9).

The New Testament does not speak of the church invisible. It always assumes the church visible! Christians have too often minimized the importance of the covenant community of believers, the church visible, by speaking of the invisible spiritual body of Christ as made up of all those who are saved. The concept of the invisible church is a man-made doctrine which claims that ultimately only God knows the heart of each person who is a genuine believer. But as disciples of Christ this is a false perspective. The church by its very nature must be visible. Those who follow Christ must openly relate their faith and ethics to the social setting in which they find themselves. We are the people of God, as Paul says, living epistles "known and read of all men" (2 Corinthians 3:2). Jesus says that whoever acknowledges Him before men He will acknowledge before the Father in heaven. (See Matthew 10:32.) It is this confession in life which makes the church visible.

Vance Havner tells of a man he invited to a revival meeting. The man declined the invitation, informing Havner that he did not belong to any congregation — he belonged to the invisible church. After further conversation, the man said that he enjoyed singing and might come to sing in the choir. Dr. Havner responded,

"You'd better find an invisible choir and sing in it."

The doctrine of the invisible church has been used by many to escape their responsibility in the church. It also robs them of sharing in a meaningful fellowship. Similarly, the emphasis on the ecumenical church has been construed by some as a way of rejecting responsible participation in the local congregation and its role in a given denomination. When we know Christ as Lord and share in the new life which He gives, we become a part of His new community in its local fellowship. Everyone who knows Christ is a brother or sister. We share a common fellowship in the Spirit.

Paul writes in Ephesians 5:25-27 that "Christ loved the church and gave himself up for her, that he might sanctify her, having cleansed her by the washing of water with the word, that he might present the church to himself in splendor, without spot or wrinkle or any such thing." This passage is one of the most striking statements underlying the disciplinary character of fellowship. Christ's purpose is to create a holy church "without spot or wrinkle," meaning (in the Greek) not even a small blemish like a freckle. Our fellowship is not simply to do things together, but to be together, to encourage one another spiritually.

True, the church is here for the needy, for us sinners, but not to leave us at ease in our sin. Rather, the church is where we help one another claim resurrection power for freedom from sin. If the church is to "be holy and without blame before him in love" (Ephesians 1:4, KJV), then we as disciples are to be holy and without blame before Him in love! For me to achieve this in even a small way, I need encouragement of my fellow believers. The life of the world is contrary to this, and only by abiding in Christ in the community of disciples can any of us live in resurrection fellowship.

The nature of this covenant of love which makes the church a community of fellowship is seen in the experience of the Last Supper with Jesus and the disciples. John shares the moving story of the Master washing His disciples' feet, teaching us that if our Lord stopped to serve in this lowly task, we should likewise serve one another. (See John 13:1-20.) John tells us that Jesus loved His own to the full extent of love. As he broke bread and shared the cup Jesus said, "This is my body which is given for you. . . . This cup which is poured out for you is the new covenant in my blood" (Luke 22:19, 20). When we share the Lord's Supper we should be expressing our covenant response to His love. In taking the bread and the cup we pledge our lives to the death for Christ and His church.

There is no greater vocation than to build the church, the fellowship of the redeemed. Whatever our respective callings may be, we share together as members of His body, each of us a significant part of the whole. It is the very spirit of love, the covenant of fellowship in one cause, that enables us to rejoice with one another in His work while each serves in his own way.

Brotherhood does not mean equalizing our service, eliminating particular callings for church leaders, pastors, evangelists, missionaries, bishops, deacons, teachers, and the like. Rather, it calls for supporting and encouraging those whose calling is different from our own. There are those who minimize callings, ordination, or commissioned leadership, by saying this is not the character of brotherhood. It appears to me to be an evidence of brotherhood or brotherliness when I can recognize the particular gifts of my brother and support him with joy, remembering that we are members of the same body of Christ.

It is in direct response to the grace of God in Christ that we in turn share the grace of the new life. Paul's classic expression of the character of this new life for the disciple is given in Romans 12. In this chapter he speaks to the Christian lifestyle in three dimensions: to one's own life (vv. 1-3), to one's life in the covenant community (vv. 4-13), and to one's life in society (vv. 14-21).

First, regarding our personal life, we are to present ourselves to God as expressions of holiness and reverence. We are to avoid conformity to the world by the renewal of our minds in the will of God. This phrase, "renewal in the spirit of your mind," calls us to humble awareness of the limitations of our own mental perspective and offers incentive for enriching the intellectual aspects of discipleship. We are to accept ourselves honestly before God, recognizing our calling.

Second, regarding our life in the covenant community, we are to respect the various gifts and callings of our fellow disciples as we work together; we are to hear and enrich one another. We are to serve in a spirit of grace, being aglow with the Spirit. In our zeal we are to outdo one another in honor, but we are to be sincere in loving one another. As a covenant community we are to support one another, especially in prayer and hospitality.

And third, regarding our life in society, we are to bless those who mistreat us and even dare to love our enemies. We are to avoid respect of persons and are to relate to the lowly. In practicing love we are to avoid repaying evil with evil, but rather live peacefully with all, overcoming evil with good. In place of revenge we are to minister to the needs of our enemies, knowing that the good deed will quicken a sense of shame and guilt for their evil. In this way evil can be overcome by good.

To walk in the resurection is to be a responsible participant in the new humanity Christ is creating. This fellowship is already demonstrating what it means to know the risen Lord transforming our lives. With this quality of life before them, faith in Christ will become an option for many of the lost in society.

Christianity does not answer the philosophies of men who oppose Christianity primarily by philosophical argument. The better answer is in the quality of the new life in Christ, in the nature of brotherhood and the character of the redeemed community. This fellowship can be the answer to Marxist materialism and its charge that religion is the opiate of the people. It can answer the challenge of Buddhism that Christianity is given to power, dominance, and violence. It can answer Western secularism by demonstrating a life of responsible interrelation with others in the experience of faith and love rather than living for selfish advantage. The world needs to see a quality of Christian brotherhood that relates and serves in the Spirit of Christ. As we "flesh out" the fellowship of Christ, His kingdom becomes visible.

The MISSIONARY PRINCIPLE

We are bought with a price – therefore . . .

9

The Missionary Principle

Who or what is a missionary? Whose job is it? Minister?

The announcement of the kingdom was the central emphasis of Jesus' proclamation. His life and works revealed the character of the kingdom. Everything that the community of disciples does in faith is an expression of the new people of God and serves to make faith an option for others. Evangelism is the total task of the total congregation. The Jesus lifestyle, the nature of the covenant community, is itself a witness in society.

In 2 Corinthians 5:18-20 Paul writes that God has given to us the ministry of reconciliation, and as agents of reconciliation, he describes us as "ambassadors for Christ." We are official representatives of our Sovereign in another land. We are representatives of Christ in as direct a relationship with Him as an ambassador is to his king or president.

Christ clearly commissioned us to make disciples. After His resurrection, Jesus said, "All authority in heaven and on earth has been given to me. Go therefore and make disciples of all nations . . . teaching them to observe all that I have commanded you; and lo, I am with you always, even to the close of the age" (Matthew 28:18-20). The risen Lord said, "You shall receive power when the Holy Spirit has come upon you; and you shall be my witnesses in Jerusalem and in all Judea and Samaria and to the end of the earth" (Acts 1:8). The missionary principle is the basic characteristic of the disciple. The life of the church is not a program but a mission.

It is strange that so few theological works on Christ give attention to the areas of evangelism and missions. Even the many treatments of the doctrine of the church address themselves far more to the interpretation of sacraments, polity, and ecumenicity than to the life and extension of the church in evangelism. It is by evangelism that the church exists, for the church is related to evangelism as effect is to cause. As Brunner has said, "The church exists by mission as fire exists by burning."[1]

It is evangelism that actually expresses the ecumenical or worldwide nature of the church. It calls Christians to affirm that commitment to Christ is more than the particular forms of identification practiced by a given denomination. But in twenty years of interdenominational, often city-wide, evangelistic crusades or preaching missions in which I have served, the liberal churches which affirm ecumenical concerns are as negative toward cooperation in evangelism as are extreme Fundamentalists. The liberals fail because they have no commitment to the *kerygma* in evangelism. The extreme Fundamentalists hesitate to cooperate lest they fail to express the *kerygma* clearly in such broader associations.

In evangelism we bear witness of Jesus Christ, not to our particular ideology. In fact, Professor Jan M. Lochman has said, "It is better to speak of the ideology of a Christian than of a Christian ideology. Ideology is the function of man, not man the function of ideology."[2] We witness of Christ, and testify of His lordship rather than insisting on our particular system of thought.

However, we must honestly recognize that there is an "ideological taint," as Reinhold Niebuhr calls it, in our expression of faith. It is simply Christian realism to be honest about this "taint." But this does not prevent our witness; rather, it calls for tolerance in relation to others. Tolerance is not indifference. A tolerant man takes his fellowman seriously and seeks interaction with him in the struggle for truth. If our faith is authentic it will seek articulation.

One reason people minimize evangelism is their lack of clarity regarding the nature and the necessity of reconciliation to Christ. Faith is response to God, to His promises and faithfulness, not simply to a system of faith about God. There is a serious danger of a faith-in-faith theology. When men interpret Christianity as a philosophy of ethics, it becomes moralism. For such persons to speak of faith as conversion is difficult. They are not so concerned about conversion to the person of Christ in covenant fellowship as they are about facilitating a moral change in life. In the latter case, persons cannot speak of conversion as a definite fact, for there are additonal changes that need to be made. They may even jest about the idea of "being saved" or of assurance of salvation. But when conversion is thought of as entering a covenant relation with the risen Christ, this is a decisive commitment — as definite as entering a covenant of marriage! This covenant results in moral change, it is true, but the covenant centers on relating to a Person rather than achieving a certain level of morality. We can speak of having been converted, of being saved, because of the definiteness of this relationship with Christ. But we dare not absolutize the act of faith itself — it is faith in God, in His promise, in His fidelity in a covenant relation that saves.

The progress of God's revelation to man, or "Salvation History"[3] as Oscar Cullmann expresses it, bringing us to the full revelation of God in Christ, introduces covenant relationship. Christian faith, or saving faith, is not just better ideas about God but is rather a covenant relation with God in Christ. We trust in Him, in His faithfulness to His covenant of promise, and faith is our participation in covenant. As disciples we have assurance of salvation, for we are committed to Him and He keeps His word.

Having referred to the dearth of materials in theology which deal with evangelism, reference should be made to some unique expressions of missionary concern by several prominent theologians. For example, when Professor Emil Brunner retired from the University of Zurich, he went to Japan to assist in missions. Another note of interest is the ministry of Professor Karl Barth who preached frequently in the prisons. An outstanding expression is the evangelical ministry of Helmut Thielicke in Hamburg, Germany. Similarly, the more significant aspect, in my judgment, of the work of the World Council of Churches has not been its attempt to promote ecumenicity, but rather those areas where it has related directly to Christian missions.

The World Congresses on Evangelism, held by

evangelical Christians beginning with Berlin in 1966, with subsequent meetings in various parts of the world and the Congress in Lausanne, Switzerland, in 1974, have contributed greatly to the understanding and work of evangelism in the Third World, and the emphasis on discipling the thousands who have come to Christ.

Evangelism is related directly to the essential nature of the covenant community or church. The church is a fellowship which one enters voluntarily, committing himself to the lordship of Christ and the brotherhood of disciples. The community, as such, will have cultural or ethnic characteristics, but these are not the essential life of the church. They may change — in fact, must change — lest they be idolized as ultimate expressions of discipleship. If a community of disciples retains patterns of the past too long, it may find itself so out of stride with the present that it cannot communicate. On the other hand, if a community of believers accommodates itself to the social order of its time in compromise of the nature of the kingdom of Christ, it will not represent the radically different nature of the new humanity Christ is creating. At the heart of the life of the community of disciples is the calling and nature of evangelism, guiding the fellowship to discover how best to communicate the lordship of Christ. [4]

Evangelism is related to the very nature of the church as the manner in which members are brought into the covenant community. Evangelism is the good news to people in the world's social order — news that there is a place for them in the kingdom of heaven. It appeals to them to consider the Christian faith and to commit themselves to Christ. As Jesus confronted men, calling them to repent, to believe, to be born anew, to come follow Him, so we as disciples of Christ call our fellowmen to repent, to come follow Christ. We never dismiss a person as an unlikely candidate for salvation!

Michelangelo went to Florence to pursue his sculpturing and found that the other artists had claimed all the choice pieces of Carrara marble — all except one cracked, misshapen piece. He studied that piece with infinite patience until he discovered how he could release the statue he had in mind. From that rejected rock he fashioned his masterpiece, *David*. So our vision in evangelism comes from what we know God can make out of misshapen lives.

But often evangelism is perverted by placing other issues above this call to covenant relation with the risen Lord. The motivation in evangelism cannot be first to "build our church." It is not first to revolutionize society. It is not first to change the economic order. Evangelism is to call men into reconciliation with Christ, to a covenant of love. This will build the congregation. In changing lives it will change society. By Christian stewardship and love for the poor and oppressed, it will work for equal opportunity for all and thereby change the economic order. While membership in the kingdom of heaven has no more direct relationship with the political order than Christ had with Pilate, the commitment of the disciple to the kingdom of the risen Christ is similar to Christ before Pilate exposing the evils of civil religion or cultural religion.

The missionary principle is the higher expression of the value of all humanity as held by Christ. Here is evidence that we love all men, that status is not a consideration in the Christian community. In the love of Christ we can say, "Blessed are you poor. We are especially interested in you. You count with us because you count with God." This involves a high percentage of the world's population of over four billion people! Not a single individual among them is unimportant. All persons are created in God's image, all have altered that image, and all are called to experience the restoration of God's image within them. Our love for others is more than sympathy for their plight. It seeks the spiritual restoration of their essential and highest personhood.

In a state church, where everyone is a member from infancy, the understanding of church can become so formalized that the meaning of covenant relation with Christ is obscured. Everyone in such a society thinks himself to be a Christian.

Evangelism is the confrontation of such persons with the call to a personal covenant with Christ. This is not simply a stimulus for personal piety, but is more significantly a personal act of covenant, of identification with Christ as Lord, of membership in His kingdom and thereby of sharing in a community of disciples.

During the last half of the 1960s in America, the work of evangelism faced a special difficulty in the revolutionary mood of young people. Christianity could likely profit from being more revolutionary in a redemptive way in society, but many youth of the

1960s were so "covenanted" to bring about change by political confrontation that this seemed to take the place of a covenant with Christ. But the first half of the 1970s has seen a remarkable change. The youth movement faced its own emptiness, discovered the same sins of status seeking and power struggle in its ranks that it rejected in society, found the counterculture too superficial, and in the honesty of youthful idealism looked for something else.

The "Jesus People" marked a new movement in America, and many enlisted. The charismatic movement won many who were looking for some evidence of experience that would attest to spiritual reality. And a new sense of revival or awakening within the church led others to take the claims of Christianity seriously. Interestingly, it was not confrontations of a philosophical or polemical nature that evangelized, so much as the expressions of newness of life by little covenant groups of the committed that won others. The response of Jewish young people to the gospel of Christ in the United States in this period is a new happening and attests to the quality of this communication. [5]

During the winter of 1974 in a visit with New Testament scholar Oscar Cullmann, he asked me about the reports of new spiritual interests and experience among the youth in America. He was more than enthusiastic about this, and shared similar word from France, Switzerland, and Germany. He mentioned the significance of this because of the secularism which has permeated European church life and thought, especially through Bultmann's influence. "The gospel of our Lord ultimately triumphs," Cullmann commented.

Similarly, the cause of missions is at the fore again. The gathering of over 14,000 college and university students at Urbana, Illinois, in December 1973, at the Inter-Varsity Missionary Conference is witness to this fact. During the same month it was my privilege to be an observer at an All-Africa Conference on Evangelism in Nairobi, sponsored by the Africa Association of Christian Churches. Here one prominent emphasis was to reinstate the word "missionary," free it from its expatriate connotations, and motivate the churches to send out missionaries, people with the Christ-mission, to share the gospel of the new life. This conference affirmed that we are beyond the days of colonialism. The national church is now filling its role to live and preach Christ among its own people who, knowing their lives, can observe the quality of the new people of God. They call for the missionary from other lands to come, to identify primarily as members of the same kingdom of Christ, and to serve not as foreign administrators but as brothers in proclamation and service.

After three extended trips in ministry in the Far East, I am confident that the day of the missionary is not past. In fact, a new day may just be dawning. This age of international representation makes possible people from a variety of cultures and nations serving in ministries to various countries as testimony to the universal nature of the kingdom of Christ. Christian disciples from the Third World may be God's best tools to evangelize in the secularized West and to call us to a renewal of Christian discipleship.

The cause of evangelism is an extension of the resurrection. It is the expression through us of Jesus' words, "All authority in heaven and on earth has been given to me. Go therefore" (Matthew 28:18, 19). The risen Lord is building His kingdom. We read of "all that Jesus began to do and teach" (Acts 1:1) and we share today in all that Jesus continues to do through His Spirit. To walk in the resurrection is to share the mission of Jesus Christ our Lord.

RELATING
to
GOVERNMENT

10

Relating to Government

"Caesar is not Lord; Jesus Christ is Lord." This was the position of the first-century church as they were pressured to conform to the civil religion of the Roman Empire. And in one way or another this has been a basic issue through the centuries. When we affirm the kingdom of heaven as a reality and the lordship of Christ as our only ultimate covenant we offend the powers of this world. But this is to stand where Jesus stood, for He said, "The ruler of this world is coming. He has no power over me" (John 14:30), and again, "My kingship is not of this world" (John 18:36).

Our relation to the civil orders, however, is not to ignore them. As disciples of Christ we live in the world; we are a part of society; we, more than others, have a vision of the ultimate potential of humanity and we care about the situation of life for every person. With Christ we too call society to repentance, even a society which in the large has lost the consciousness of sin. We are responsible first to live in society with moral responsibility, and then to call society to both individual and social accountability.

Christian faith is not religious sacraments to which one turns on Sunday to resolve the guilts of the week. It is rather living each day in the will of God. As Jesus said, "Seek first his kingdom and his righteousness, and all these things shall be yours as well" (Matthew 6:33). Nor is Christian discipleship a way of life for a select few. Rather, it is the calling for all of us to deny ourselves, take up the cross daily, and follow Christ. It is in being disciples of Jesus in society that we call men and women to confess Christ and share the fellowship of His kingdom. This is the prophetic role of the people of God in society.

It is refreshing to find such voices in America today as Senator Mark Hatfield of Oregon and psychiatrist Karl Menninger calling America to repentance. Senator Hatfield warns, "Our civil religion places our nation beyond sin and above judgment. It baptizes nationalistic vainglory. We abdicate our individual responsibility and the dictates of our personal faith to corporate idolatry. We can see this in the religious realm where the integrity of our faith is compromised by civil religion and political when idolatry of power overcomes individual convictions."[1] And from his field of psychiatry Dr. Menninger says, "There is immorality. There is unethical behavior. There is wrongdoing. And I hope to show that there is usefulness in retaining the concept and indeed the word, sin."[2]

These statements support the emphasis on the role of the Christian disciple as a witness to Christian integrity in society. In a world of secularism we must help the secularist discover that there is more to reality than human achievements, and in thought and social achievement we must keep secular society from claiming wholeness for itself. As members of the kingdom of Christ we introduce society to a new humanity, stimulating within it the dawning of faith. Society needs its structures, social and political; we do not negate these, for they are ordered by God. But neither do we idolize them nor obey them in the place of God. In Romans 13:1, Paul says that God has ordained the governing authorities for our well-being. However, we should note that when he says, "There is no authority except from God" it is clear that God is above government! By obedience to our Lord we have no fear of the government needing to administer punishment to us. On the other hand, in obeying our Lord we do not look to the government for guidance in morality. The rulers of this world do not set our standard.

Walking in the resurrection is to live as a new humanity, to live by a standard which finds its norm in Jesus Christ, who in His resurrection introduced us to the ultimate humanity in which we share. Of this Carl F. H. Henry says, "The risen Christ demonstrates in His person the character of humanity God approves in the eternal order; His is the moral image to which all the people of God will ultimately be conformed."[3] We are called to this newness in the covenant community, and in this relationship we join hands with fellow disciples around the world who affirm the kingdom of Christ.

The beginning point for the expression of discipleship is in the family. In our homes we can express what it means to be a new people of God, and in doing so influence the next generation to extend His kingdom. Our calling is to be truly Christian at home, with those we love in a unique way, with those who are especially near to us. In Christ we experience a mental and spiritual wholeness which contributes to the quality of all our relationships. In marriage and the family we share in the joys of love and fellowship, in the security of trust and belonging. The home is to be an expression of our covenant together with Christ. To such a covenant Paul refers in his mention of "the church in their house" (Romans 16:5 and 1 Corinthians 16:19). While family life varies because of the different patterns of personalities which make up different homes, each family can know the integrity of love and trust.

The new people of God have a special witness to give for the integrity of love in marriage amidst the proliferation of divorce, sexual infidelity, and status seeking which destroy the family. In marriage Christian disciples do not dodge the problems which arise from differences and seek to escape them in divorce; rather, we take them as challenges to mature in those graces needed for harmony. Children need to know how much we love them even as we correct them.

A happy family is an honest family, even though this means working through difficulties rather than pretending they do not exist. The social order can be refined and enriched through the development of quality families more thoroughly than by any other medium in society. Yet the spirit of our times attacks the integrity of the home as frontally as any issue. Here is where the disciple begins in working for renewal and calling for repentance.

One of the greater problems confronting the home is the breakdown of togetherness due to our economic and social patterns of life. Husband and wife do far too little together as partners. Because of their professional roles most of their time is spent with others and their ability to communicate with each other is hindered. Vacations for a family are not a luxury; they are an essential part of strengthening family ties.

In parent-child relationships there is little opportunity for parents and children to work together, to associate in the normal experiences of life. As a consequence, their interaction can easily become artificial and forced. Most of the talking may take place in connection with disagreements and discipline. Youth spend the bulk of their time with other young people no more experienced nor mature than themselves. One of my deepest frustrations is that the lifestyle of our youth is shaped more by the influence of others whose experience is so limited rather than by a responsible family relationship. In Colossians 3:18-25, where Paul writes about walking in the resurrection, he addresses the family specifically regarding the character of the new life.

It is with respect to the importance and problems of maintaining strong family life that the fellowship of the church or covenant community is especially relevant. Partners need other associates for fellowship, and they can best find this fellowship in the church. The children, even more, must have a circle of friends for their social life and development. They need others in addition to their parents to add breadth and authenticity to their understanding of the meaning of faith. The community of disciples, as a genuine expression of the new humanity, is the ideal frame of reference for the developing person. The congregation of believers is responsible to create those effective functions which will both educate and enhance the maturity of its members.

A major part of our intellectual and social development takes place in the educational process. The Christian community, whatever the educational program of a given culture, must provide for a valid presentation of the Christian perspective. The Christian family and the church must not abdicate responsibility in education and leave this to the secular order. In many countries scholastic achievement by Christians qualifies them for faculty positions in the educational system. In America, with its unique pattern of private colleges, many operated by Christian churches, there is opportunity for the development of the Christian school in perspective and spirit.

Christian education is simply education from the stance of a Christian world-view. Education is always approached from some perspective, and the Christian philosophy is as valid as any other in the development of an educational pattern. No one can master the wealth of knowledge in the world today. Consequently, all educational programs are selective in the information and analysis they pursue. A Christian world-view in education will integrate the sacred and the secular, and will incorporate the broadest possible understandings of the world's cultures and peoples. Education is Christian insofar as the interpretation makes clear the basis for Christian faith as an option.

But education is more than transmission of knowledge; it is the pursuit of an understanding and an experience of meaning. The Christian in education is not dealing only with information, but with life itself. When we educate from the perspective of the new people of God, the new humanity Christ is creating, the educational process must introduce the student to both the possibilities and the character of this humanity. Whatever the school context, Christian education will have about it the character of covenant community — a fellowship of disciples who seek to know and live the truth as it is in Jesus.

A Christian education will take seriously the character and need of humanity itself. It will deal responsibly with philosophy and ethics to achieve a clear understanding of human relationships. It will pursue the behavioral sciences, art, and history for knowledge and appreciation of humanness. It will engage itself in the various fields of the natural sciences for the service of mankind, especially in the frontal areas of ecology, food production, health, and the understanding of physiological factors that affect various world cultures. A Christian education will prepare persons to give themselves in the spirit of Jesus Christ to serve for the benefit of mankind around the world.

Education today must be global in its awareness and relationships. All mankind is our field. The kingdom of Christ is global, and our covenant as Christians includes fellow disciples in every land and culture. The Third World is especially significant at this point, for here the stirrings of humanity are expressed by their reaching for the meanings and privileges of the more technologically advanced peoples. It is the responsibility of Christians in education to see that persons from the Third World come to understand more than technological developments, finding basic Christian meanings as well. For many in the Third World, issues of meaning have been more frontal than technology. Because of this, identification with the values of the Christian faith may be easier for them to accept than many aspects of secularization. Additionally, we now have the Fourth World, Arab countries, which provide us with still more opportunities for understanding, dialogue, and demonstrating Christian love.

As disciples of Christ, we should know the meaning of nonconformity to secularism. Paul writes, "Do not be conformed to this world" (Romans 12:2), or as Phillips translates it, "Don't let the world squeeze you into its mold." This does not mean that I am not a man with other men, a person who belongs in society, who is a part of humanity. The incarnation means "the Word become flesh," that God affirmed humanness in Jesus Christ, and as His disciples we are participants in humanness as He intended it. Being new creatures in Christ, walking in the resurrection, means that we are participants in the new humanity, in that fellowship which makes us truly human. Our nonconformity to the world comes from this essential change of our own persons. We are different because God is restoring His image within us.

Nonconformity to the world in a biblical sense involves more than simply being different from the world, more than adopting a different lifestyle which we can structure culturally. Our nonconformity is dependent upon "our being transformed by the renewing of our minds, our demonstrating the will of God in our person" (Romans 12:2, paraphrase). This means that our norm, the criteria for our lifestyle, is identification with the risen Lord. It is not to watch how society moves and then simply to do it differently.

Nonconformity will create a relationship between the church and society of mutual criticism; we will speak to each other and hear each other. Not only do we have something to say in witness to society, but we need to hear what society has to say to us, for it can challenge us to be true to our profession. In fact, the challenge by society keeps the church from becoming just another organization of power in the social milieu. A basic aspect of our nonconformity to secularism is to take the towel and basin, as our Master did, and wash our brother's feet.

This spirit of life is in direct contrast to the use of violence in our society, one of the cornerstones of modern civilization. On the one hand, Marxism has an ideology that claims to understand history and that will use any means, including violence, to achieve its goal, believing that the end justifies the means. On the other hand, the so-called free world has similarly used violence as its means to the end of preserving our freedom.

How different the words of Jesus sound: "Love your enemies, do good to those who hate you, and pray for those who misuse you. Be perfect in love as your Father is perfect" (Matthew 5:44-48, paraphrase). Or Paul's words, "Beloved, never avenge yourselves, but leave it to the wrath of God; for it is written, 'Vengeance is mine, I will repay, says the Lord.' No, 'if your enemy is hungry, feed him; if he is thirsty, give him drink. . . . "Do not be overcome by evil, but overcome evil with good" (Romans 12:19-21). Or again, in Romans 13:8, 10, he writes, "Owe no one anything, except to love one another; for he who loves his neighbor has fulfilled the law. . . . Love does no wrong to a neighbor; therefore love is the fulfilling of the law." The way of love confronts the very cornerstone of this world's civilization with another way of life, the spirit of the new humanity.

Since much violence has to do with property, either to gain possession at the expense of others or in protecting what one has rightfully acquired, our attitude toward the material is an essential aspect of this issue. First, we must always affirm the ultimate value of human personality above mere things. And second, we should never ask anyone to give his life for our things. We can adjust our expectations to live without things, but we cannot replace lives that have been lost.

For social and economic reasons society is organized into political orders. And these orders in the various forms of government are valid as long as they have the good of the citizen at heart. When they become despotic and use the people for the advantage of the "ruling class," they are perverted. In view of this, the church in any society must both witness to the government to be true to its calling, and hear the government speak to it lest the church become a governing body rather than a redemptive fellowship and in so doing be untrue to its calling. The government by its nature should be secular, and let the church be the church. As Franklin Littell of Temple University has said, "A secular government is a good government, a secular church is a rotten church." [4]

When government functions in God's plan for

government it will punish the evil and protect the good. It will order society in a way that safeguards the good and the freedom of its citizens. It will enhance the cultural, educational, social, and moral aspects of life by promoting the best creative interests of its people, seeking the privileges of equal opportunity and the development of all citizens, safeguarding their freedom for personal fulfillment, and protecting their right to that freedom. When these things are threatened by internal disorder and violence, the Scripture says of government that it "does not bear the sword in vain" (Romans 13:4). When this is threatened from without, government has the responsibility to negotiate for its people to achieve understanding and when necessary to protect its highest level of moral judgment.

The witness of the Christian church in society is to point to the highest level of moral judgment as we know it in Christ. We add our voice to the many others to promote a more Christian ethic in social and political matters. As Menno Simons said, "He who is a Christian must follow the Spirit, Word, and example of Christ, no matter whether he be emperor, king, or whatever he be. For these following admonitions apply to all alike: 'Let this mind be in you which was also in Christ Jesus.' Philippians 2:5. 'He that saith he abideth in Him ought himself also so to walk, even as He walked.' 1 John 2:6."[5]

But obviously, government cannot speak and act for each of its citizens even while it acts for all of them. And it cannot act for the church. As disciples of Christ, we are first members of another kingdom. We have a mission of redemptive relationship with all men which calls us to action in the Spirit of Christ. This is not less but more demanding, and means that the Christian lives with a mission of reconciliation and follows the path of nonresistance to evil in that mission, while its government may take a course altogether different — anything but a course of pacifism. But the Christian disciple reaches his hand to fellow disciples in other parts of the world, enhancing understanding of the problem and the basis for negotiation. The disciple does not find his security in the nationalism of his land and in its military strength, but in the cause of Christ who calls him to live in love for the world.

This is not to be less loyal to one's nation. But having this universal perspective means that we serve our nation for its good as we serve Christ in the new humanity He is creating. The Australian evangelist, Alan Walker, says that history will be dated pre-Vietnam and post-Vietnam because of the general conviction in the world that war is wrong and is no solution for the human problem. [6]

In the sixteenth century Menno Simons, a strong evangelical leader, emphasized the necessity of personal conversion, a believers' church, and a personal experience of the indwelling of the Holy Spirit and a life of discipleship. He spoke to the issue of war and peace as it relates to the teachings of Christ. If the Christian church, worldwide, could heed this and put evangelism and brotherhood at the fore, we could do more to change the world for the better than war for so-called "just causes" has ever done. He said, "The regenerated do not go to war, nor engage in strife.

They are the children of peace who have beaten their swords into plowshares and their spears into pruning hooks, and know of no war. . . . Since we are to be conformed to the image of Christ, how can we then fight our enemies with the sword? . . . Spears and swords of iron we leave to those who, alas, consider human blood and swine's blood of well-nigh equal value. . . ."[7]

But the basic issue is not whether all Christians can be brought to a position of conscientious objection to war, nor whether we can achieve a position on the part of government that will limit conscription and have only a voluntary army. The basic issue is whether the Christian church can see its role as qualitatively different from that of the state, and, by seeing separation of church and state in the dimension of character and purpose, affirm its membership as first in the kingdom of Christ and express this by working for peace.

The path of nonresistance is the way of the future. Christians of all nations can affirm their brotherhood and demonstrate true fellowship. At the same time they can avoid becoming a church establishment which attempts to govern society (the proper role of government, not of the church). The more clearly these roles are kept separate, the greater will be the respect for Christian ideals on the part of society itself.

When people perpetuate the myth of a Christian state they obscure the distinction that I am making. But when we call the church to be church and the state to be the state, the church or covenant community can go about its calling of being a new humanity, a people of God in the world but not of it. This means that we regard the covenant community as a discipling minority. It lives in the world as a pilgrim people, a people whose confession of the lordship of Christ governs every relationship.

Those who seek a Christian state seek to order the life of the total society by their Christian idealism, and must in so doing try to provide a Christian ethic for the state. But our calling as disciples of Christ is not to outline an ethic for the world, but to live by the love ethic of Christ amidst the world. When we "render to Caesar the things that are Caesar's (Luke 20:25) we must be careful that we render only that, lest we render to Caesar that which we are to render only to God.

An interesting story comes out of the early eighteenth century of an interchange between King Charles XII of Sweden and a Mennonite preacher of Prussia. During the siege of Thorn in 1703 King Charles, hearing that Stephen Funk, a Mennonite preacher, was teaching peace and nonviolence as the way for the Christian, sent for him and brought him to the military camp. Asking if it was true that Funk was teaching nonresistance, he requested Funk to preach for them and prove his point from the Bible. Following the sermon, King Charles asked if Funk meant that war is unconditionally condemned in the Scriptures. After a bit of thought, Funk answered, " 'If anything could be allowed in the Holy Scriptures, it might be that a king who is attacked in his own realm might defend himself, but that a king march into another realm to conquer and devastate it, for that there is no freedom in the Scriptures; on the contrary, it is absolutely opposed to Christ's teachings." [8]

But does this mean that the Christian disciple, who lives as a pacifist as Jesus did, can be regarded as a parasite in society? Do we as members of the kingdom of heaven live at the expense of, or on the sacrifice of, others? In one sense, all humanity is bound together "in the bundle of life" and none of us lives apart from the service of others. But in a specific manner the disciple of Christ who lives as a member of the kingdom of heaven is called to give his total life in service for the benefit of others. If we are true to our calling, we will be involved in many services of education, ecology, poverty, health, management, and the like, which are needed by our fellowman. We will give ourselves to the more needy and difficult areas of human problems. We will own and use property as stewards for the cause of Christ, but not ask that others die to protect it for us. Rather, what is "mine" may even be taken by the government when necessary to fulfill its calling. As a disciple of Christ, beyond respecting and praying for my government, it is my privilege to serve to the death in other ministries of love. I can delight in helping the downtrodden. I can devote my energies to bringing freedom to the oppressed, healing to the suffering and broken, encouragement to those who despair of their lot in society, and extending fellowship to all that may discover that each of us is made in the image of God and that this image can be restored.

Our relation to the powers, who tend to the idolatry of power itself, is not one of condemnation, but of emancipation. In each period of Christian history it has always been the witness of free men who answer to the lordship of Christ which has confronted the powers with their own finitude. Jesus stood before Pilate with bound hands, but He was not "bound" to speak as Pilate asked. And when He spoke, it was of a kingdom of truth and freedom, a rule that would create new men. He demonstrated what He taught: "The kings of the earth lord it over their subjects, but it shall not be among you, for I am among you as one who serves" (Luke 22:25-27, paraphrase). For one who confesses Christ as Lord, the desire to rule is wrong. We are to love our neighbor as ourselves. (See Mark 12:28-31).

GOD
and
MAMMON

11

God and Mammon

"Christianity is the most materialistic religion in the world," said William Temple.[1] The reason? Because it takes the material order seriously. As disciples we do not withdraw from life to be more holy. But as we have seen, the grace of God restores to us a true humanness in the renewal of His image within us. Just as the Incarnation is God's great affirmation of humanness, and the resurrection His expression of the eternal pattern for the humane, so we find His call for us to live in holiness as a quality of life in the midst of the material order. God makes us true persons in society, not persons withdrawn from society.

This corresponds to another unique aspect of Christianity — its historicity. God has acted in the stream of history, disclosing a revelation of Himself, creating a people, meeting us above all in the Son of Man, Jesus Christ, acting in the Holy Spirit through His church. This very historicity is related to God's affirmation of the created order, which is the expression of His creative providence. History has meaning and movement; history is going somewhere! God has promised that Christ will return to introduce the church to its ultimate reign with Him, to judge the nations of the world, and to liberate the world from the perversion imposed upon it by man's sin.

As disciples of Christ, we already share the meaning of the future. We live now in the flush of dawn which announces the new day. How then shall we regard the material world with which we have to do? Peter writes, "Since all these things are thus to be dissolved, what sort of persons ought you to be in lives of holiness and godliness?" (2 Peter 3:11). The decisions of the present should be controlled by our ultimate goal. The esteemed Mennonite churchman, Paul Erb, has said, "A pilgrim people need a pilgrim ethic." One who already walks in the resurrection will "hang loose" with respect to the things of the world. As Menno Simons wrote of the disciples of Christ, "Their kingdom is a kingdom of grace, here in hope and after this in eternal life. Their citizenship is in heaven, and they use the lower creations with thanksgiving and to the necessary support of their own lives, and to the free service of their neighbor, according to the Word of God." [2]

We live, in confessing Christ as Lord, "in the world but not of it," but also "using it but not abusing it." It is the tension created by "using and not abusing" which creates the difficulty for us. But at the same time this is the essential strength of the disciple's stance in the economic orders. To be free in Christ means to stand in freedom from the tyranny of things as well as to know freedom in relationships.

Jesus spoke to this in the Sermon on the Mount, asking us to trust the Father's care rather than to be anxious about material things. Our security is in the promise of God with respect to the benefits of the natural life as well as the spirit. Security is not in nature. The birds live with a cycle of life which is constant enough to meet their needs for tomorrow, and we who know God and can think of Him as they cannot should so much the more trust God.[3] The basic problem is that concern about material things perverts and robs us of involvement in building the kingdom of Christ. When Jesus said, in Matthew 19:24, that "it is easier for a camel to go through the eye of a needle than for a rich man to enter the kingdom of God," He was no doubt speaking about involvement in the work of the kingdom of God now.

Christian stewardship means that one's property is under the lordship of Christ, first of all an asset for the kingdom, not for oneself. This is expressed beautifully by a sixteenth-century Anabaptist:

> Nobody can inherit the kingdom unless he is poor with Christ, for a Christian has nothing of his own; no place where he can lay his head. A real Christian should not even have enough property on earth to be able to stand on it with one foot. This does not mean that he should not have fields and meadows, or that he should not work, but alone that he might not think they are for his own use and be tempted to say: this house is mine, this field is mine, this dollar is mine. Rather he should say it is ours, even as we pray: Our Father. In summary, a Christian should not have anything of his own but should have all things in common with his brother, *i.e.*, not allow him to suffer need. In other words, I will not work that my house be filled, that my larder be supplied with meat, but rather I will see that my brother has enough, for a Christian looks more to his neighbor than to himself. Whoever desires to be rich in this world, who is concerned that he miss nothing when it comes to his person and property, who is honored by men and feared by them, who refuses to prostrate himself at the feet of his Lord . . . will be humbled.[4]

This tension between building the kingdom and building an estate is illustrated in Luke 12:13-15 by the man who asked Jesus to negotiate for him with a brother about dividing their inheritance. Jesus' response was quite abrupt: "Man, who made me a judge or divider over you?" He told the man to discover the higher goal of building the kingdom. Is this to say that we are to be careless about material matters, or rather, that they are to be kept at the proper level?

The rich young ruler in Mark 10:17-22 indicated that he found personal satisfaction in keeping the commandments and in living an upright life. Jesus met him where he was. In answer to his question of what more to do, Jesus told him to sell what he had, give to the poor, and follow Christ. But possessions were his god. The God whose commandments he claimed to obey was not at the center of his life. Wealth was.

This god is not so easily removed as some of the lesser gods men have designed. We in the Western world are involved in the idolatry of things whereas in some other cultures the idol may be an image. Some time ago my wife and I received a letter from Laurence Horst, a missionary friend in Ghana. Relating the news of the recent baptism of nearly fifty persons into the Christian church, he gave this account:

> One brother, after baptism, said he needed help to take his god away. Could we come Saturday evening to assist him? We decided the church should help and suggested we do it Sunday morning. And so, after the baptismal service, sermon, and communion service, we all went to his compound. Someone brought an axe. I had the honor of taking the first whack at the idol. Then another person,

> and another person, and another until he looked helpless indeed. Three men turned the image over, and there was a live toad. Imagine their excitement. They killed the toad and threw it into the bush. We stood around the dethroned god and sang hymns, then had prayer for the man that he would put his whole trust in Jesus Christ. Then we each took portions of the fallen god and made a parade into the bush singing, "Onward, Christian Soldiers," and we threw him away.

What a dramatic and interesting account! But not necessarily different from what Jesus asked of the rich young man with respect to his god of wealth. And not as different as we might think from the Western world, where our god is the security of things. Our affluence without a sharing love hides the gospel from many in the world.

In early April 1974, I was on the campus of the American University, Beirut, Lebanon. For a few days prior to my arrival there had been student demonstrations on campus, shutting down normal operations. As our little group of visitors came to the gate, we had to gain entrance by negotiating with a core of student guards. As we walked through the campus, we read the numerous placards criticizing Western imperialism. One of them was a play on Jesus' words of the abundant life, and read, "I am come that you might have money and have it more abundantly." And this was on a campus which was itself an attempt to share, but being institutional could hardly communicate anything more than paternalism.

The real problem is not in the thing, but in the "thinker." Jesus did not ask Nicodemus to sell what he had. Nicodemus' problem was different. He was doing things to get to God and needed to stop long enough to let God do something for him. He needed to be born again. It was not things which had become his god, but confidence in his own works. When the person himself is changed, when he becomes a participant in the new humanity Christ is creating, his relation toward material things changes also.

The question is whether we can be good stewards. It takes a transformed life to handle material wealth for the glory of God, just as it takes a transformed life to handle other wealth properly, such as the wealth of education, talent, personality, and position. Being a steward of what is entrusted to us, of gifts the Holy Spirit has given us, is one of the most crucial tests of our commitment to Christ. When someone touches what I have, my reaction tells whether I am letting God be God, or whether I am playing god over what I have. The dynamic of tithing is that it makes a conscious partnership with God a consideration in every enterprise. This is a dimension which socialism itself does not include. It is easy to talk about the plight of the oppressed, and how the "haves" should share with the "have-nots," while at the same time failing to tithe and share from what we have.

We are responsible to God for what we do with the things which we own. And this is also where a subtle danger lies. As soon as we own property we tend to be god over what we own. When we decide what we do with what we have without letting Christ be Lord in this area we are guilty of idolatry. This is why Jesus said in Matthew 19:24 that it is nearly impossible to be rich and to be in the kingdom of heaven. Even if one declares that his wealth is not his master, he may be overlooking the fact that the nature of the idolatry is not in the wealth, but in himself. He plays god over what he has. The only safeguard in owning property is a planned partnership with God.

Can one be free of the sin of materialism as he works with what he owns? We can begin the experience of freedom by confessing this tendency to Christ, for the very act of confessing brings Him into this sphere of life. We can confess the ultimate ownership as God's, taking our place as a steward for our Lord. This is where the test of surrender becomes most personal. Will I let the Christ I confess as Lord truly be Lord in my life? With respect to things, the choice is not at all abstract. Nor is it an area of ambivalence. Jesus simply says, "You cannot serve God and mammon" (Matthew 6:24). With our confession that Christ is Lord even in the area of our finances, we can begin a deliberate plan of sharing.

But the greater answer to the problem of relating to material things is not negation. God did not negate the world when He came in Jesus Christ; the Incarnation placed Him in the world. But the world is under Him; it is not partner with Him. Similarly, He calls us to have dominion over the created order under Him. What prevents us from playing god with this assignment? The basic fact that we are functioning under God, confessing His lordship in our work, releases us to be partners with God in His creative work. The famous painting, "The Angelus," pictures the workers at the close of the day praying in the field before leaving for home.

How important that we recapture the awareness that work can be participation with God in His providence in the creative necessities of life.

This provides an important perspective for business, calling us to be partners with God. The answer to the question of the disciple's relation to material things is hardly voluntary poverty for all of us, great as was the example of St. Francis, but rather stewardship. Our work can be done with prayer that will lead to the encouragement and development of the capacities of each person to whom we relate. The disciple who senses a call to use his gifts in business enterprise can function to help humanity rather than advance himself both by the choice of what he produces and by providing jobs for many who may not be as gifted to manage a business, but who need a source of income.

Some propose communal living, or community of goods, as a Christian lifestyle. I have no doubt but that one can be a Christian disciple living with that pattern. But such a person may face problems in relating to the larger society to communicate Christ; he may be tempted to surrender to group security; he may find it difficult to maximize the full potential for development for each person in the group. I admit that I have a bias toward a free congregational life in which we cultivate stewardship and sharing with the brotherhood for the good of all.

But this position has problems, too, as I have stated — of playing god over things, of idolizing status in the group, of too little discipline by the covenant community to help us avoid affluence, and of acquiring things rather than sharing. Paul writes that one who shares the new life will "work with his hands, so that he may be able to give to those in need" (Ephesians 4:28). It is persons who are ultimately important, both in working and as the object of our giving. A Christian steward who shares in the covenant community will live with the philosophy that what's mine is really the people of God's when my brother has need!

While property is important as a trust from God, it is not as important as people. Underlying violence and war is the problem of ownership of property. True, as a Christian I am responsible for what is entrusted to me. However, property is to be used! People are not to be used. People are an end in themselves. I could not ask anyone to give his life for my property, nor to take life to protect my property. Some would place defense of their wife's virtue and the defense of their property in the same category. But as Paul says in Ephesians 5:28, she is an extension of myself in a way that property is not.

Property is to be used for God's purpose in history. It is our indifference at a level of sharing that exposes our guilt. Senator Mark Hatfield writes of the sin associated with poverty in our nation: "The poorest one-fifth of families in America receive only five percent of our nation's total family income. The wealthiest one-fifth of our society in America receive forty-two percent of the total family income. This fact has not changed in twenty-five years."[5] Millions in our own land are hungry, not to speak of the larger, worldwide problem.

In contrast to the pattern of St. Francis, the approach of the disciple in this period of history could well be to engage in the business of food production and distribution, in ecology and the training of persons for the best production and management for the needs of the world. Helping the poor and the hungry is part of our mission for Christ. In His words, "As you did it to one of the least of these my brethren, you did it to me" (Matthew 25:40).

God judges our failure to share. In the Old Testament, the Prophet Ezekiel is especially searching: "This was the guilt of your sister Sodom: she and her daughters had pride, surfeit of food, and prosperous ease, but did not aid the poor and needy" (Ezekiel 16:49). The Apostle John says, "If any one has the world's goods and sees his brother in need, yet closes his heart against him, how does God's love abide in him? Little children, let us not love in word or speech but in deed and in truth" (1 John 3:17, 18). And "He who does not love does not know God; for God is love. . . . If any one says, 'I love God,' and hates his brother, he is a liar; for he who does not love his brother whom he has seen, cannot love God whom he has not seen" (1 John 4:8, 20). One who experiences the new humanity in Christ shares His love and partakes of the fruit of the Spirit which is love. This is a new humanity in society, of which Jesus said, "By this all men will know that you are my disciples, if you have love for one another" (John 13:35).

Since society is oriented so basically to economic matters, what the disciple does with his property is a matter of witness. From Barnabas to the present, to share freely, to give without strings, to demonstrate Christian freedom over things has been a witness which speaks of a new nature. How we handle our property, as a trust from God, as stewards of something that is a part of ongoing history, is a witness to the integrity of faith. The disciple looks at ecological concerns, not just from the perspective of his own security in the universe, but as part of his responsibility under God as a steward, as a concern of both love and hope for the generations yet to come who should have a "good" world in which to participate in life.

Our ecological concerns, like our work ethic, is directly related to eschatology. We believe that there is a future which we share with Christ, that this future is in His hands, and that He has given us the mandate to occupy until He comes. Eschatological hope also involves the created order, and since the material world has a place in God's plan for the future we defy the demonic tendencies which exploit it. (See Romans 8:18-25.) To walk in the resurrection is to live freely in the world under the lordship of Christ — using but not abusing it.

"No one can serve two masters" (Matthew 6:24). With these words Jesus calls us to decision. Our loyalty cannot be divided and still achieve His goals for the kingdom. But it is this very ambivalence of divided loyalty which dulls the cutting edge of the church in society. Diplomacy, the art of getting along with both worlds, is not the primary character of discipleship. Rather, we are admonished to live by love so that the clarity of our loyalty will not be hidden and at the same time will not be abrasive in its expression. As John writes, "No man has ever seen God; if we love one another, God abides in us and his love is perfected in us" (1 John 4:12). The knowledge of God and the love of God are bound together in our expression of covenant—love to our fellows. This is the breakthrough of the resurrection life.

LED
by the
SPIRIT of JESUS

12

Led by the Spirit of Jesus

To walk in the resurrection is to walk in the Spirit. God, by the Spirit, raised Jesus from the dead. This same Spirit works in us who believe. By His presence and power we may experience fullness of life in Christ. (See Ephesians 3:14-21.) Identifying with Christ, we follow His leading. One of the most striking statements in Acts of the Apostles is the expression, "It has seemed good to the Holy Spirit and to us" (15:28). In this phrase the affirmation of life in the Spirit comes to concrete expression. The church, in its decisions, was being led by the Spirit of Jesus.

The church is His, not ours. A covenant people belong to the Lord of the covenant. A covenant community is guided by His very presence, by the Spirit of Jesus. In John 14:18 Jesus promised, "I will not leave you desolate; I will come to you." His presence keeps the church from being simply another social organization. The Spirit creates the fellowship of Christ. At Pentecost He created a new community, a new people bound to each other in a covenant of love, an expression of the life of Christ. But when the Spirit is ignored by the church, its program becomes a purely human operation. It tries to function by principles borrowed from the gospel but finds itself lacking the spirit of the gospel. The Scripture says, "Where the Spirit of the Lord is, there is freedom" (2 Corinthians 3:18).

The Christ who is Lord of history and Lord of the Scripture is also Lord of the church. Not only has He purchased the church with His own blood (Acts 20:28), but He also acts to "present the church to himself in splendor, without spot or wrinkle" (Ephesians 5:27). He stands as Judge of the church as well as Redeemer, correcting and refining the fellowship. In Revelation 2 and 3 we are given seven examples of Jesus as Judge of the church, exposing compromises and calling for repentance. The Holy Spirit disciplined the church in Acts 5, exposing the sin of Ananias and Sapphira. (See also Paul's exposure of Peter's compromise with the legalists at Antioch in Galatians 2:11-21.) Many Christians seem to seek a pious, chummy relationship with the Holy Spirit, minimizing the fact that as God is present in our lives, He is also Judge of our spirit and behavior. This should inspire the reverence asked of Moses when he drew near the bush that burned and was not consumed. God said, "Put off your shoes from your feet, for the place on which you are standing is holy ground" (Exodus 3:5).

A sense of holy reverence will open the way for further guidance from God. In our piety, we must guard against trying to manage our "spiritual" experiences, with God serving us. God is not to be manipulated. To walk in the resurrection is to move beyond the former dictates of the flesh and to share the life in which Christ is Lord, providing in His own way the insight, love, and joy of a life made whole.

To be led of the Spirit strikes at the very core of our self-confidence and our inner being. He asks us to surrender our trust in the wisdom of our natural mind and share in "the mind of Christ" (1 Corinthians 2:16). This is not easy; it takes strength to surrender. We must trade the little realms in which we can maintain control for the larger realms where we find our security in Christ.

Paul contrasts the wisdom of our humanness and the wisdom of Christ which He imparts to His new creation. This wisdom is not static. It is not given as acquired knowledge, experienced as His leading. His anointing for insight in the Word, so that we can understand spiritual things, is not static. (See 1 John 2:20.) It is mediated as we open ourselves prayerfully to Him. His gifts of grace are not static, but mediated as we covet for each occasion the best gift, for the glory of Christ. None of us is so pious that we can presume on a level of spirituality to which God has brought us. Rather, we know the meaning of abiding in Christ who said, "Apart from me you can do nothing" (John 15:5).

It follows that to be led by the Spirit is not static either.[1] None of us can presume to have His ready-made answers for each decision simply because we have known the Holy Spirit in our lives. We can be certain that His leading will correspond with what we know of the will of God in Christ Jesus, but we cannot institutionalize this. The subtle danger of routineness besets those of us who have lived and worked in the Spirit for some time.

In Acts 16:6-10 we observe that Paul, who was led

of the Spirit, could not presume to have a final sense of leading on where he was to serve until it was confirmed by the Sprit. This calls for a humility that will lay one's sense of leading before the fellowship of believers for testing. The Spirit works in the covenant community, and He will attest to His will. When Paul and Barnabas were sent on their mission of evangelism, as the covenant community worshiped and fasted, "The Holy Sirit said, 'Set apart for me Barnabas and Saul for the work to which I have called them' " (Acts 13:2). We are His agents, engaged in His work, fulfilling His mission.

For many years I have witnessed to the reality and joy of the indwelling and infilling of the Holy Spirit. For me this is an experience of personal relation with the Holy Spirit beyond my conversion, an experience that has not been static. His dynamic presence has enabled me to seek and enjoy fresh and new dimensions of relationship with Him. It also lets me accept those periods of less exhilarating relationship without the fear that I have "lost the experience." His presence with me enables me to open myself to Him again for renewal. Through these years on numerous occasions I have been so certain of His leading personally that I have acted on that basis alone. But in most cases, I have tested His leading with my wife and with others in the covenant of fellowship. The Spirit is not creating individualists even though He gives us each individuality; He is creating a body, with each of us being members of the whole.

I have discovered afresh the importance of Christian fellowship not only because each of us needs other believers to enrich our lives, but because it is one of the greater witnesses of the Spirit. When He creates — amidst an individualistic, competitive, status-seeking society — a fellowship of believers who are truly a covenant community of love and understanding, this is a frontal witness of the new humanity Jesus brings into being. The Spirit acts within the community of believers. There in worship, prayer, praise, and sharing, the Spirit can express Himself without having some "loner" pervert His expression. The gifts of the Spirit are for the brotherhood, for the enriching of this covenant community — and, in turn, for their ministry to others. They are not expressions some individual takes upon himself to personify the full expression of the Spirit. To be led of the Spirit depends upon our sharing the new life, the resurrection life, which He is creating in a covenant community of disciples.

This does not exclude personal infilling of the Spirit. The baptism with the Spirit, which is given by Jesus Christ to His disciples, is a personal experience of coming under the control of the Holy Spirit. The indwelling of the Spirit is a personal dimension of His presence in our lives, enriching, transforming, and enabling. His infilling for insight, for freedom and victory, for grace and love, is personal. Each of us must be able to say, "This is my experience." When we meet with the covenant fellowship we bring with us all that we are experiencing of God, And in the fellowship of this covenant group, we experience further infillings of the Spirit. In Acts we read that the same disciples who were personally filled with the Spirit met with fellow believers. "And when they had prayed, the place in which they were gathered together was shaken; and they were all filled [again] with the Holy Spirit and spoke the word of God with boldness" (Acts 4:31).

How can Christians know the will of Jesus for discipleship in different times and cultures? In our time, with Christian brothers of many nations in easy view, we face a great variety of cultural situations in which discipleship is to be expressed. Can some official group legislate a minimal code for Christian conduct for all? Is there a single suitable Christian lifestyle applicable for every culture? Or is the proper lifestyle of the Christian simply to be open to the leading of the Spirit of Jesus in the covenant community? Such a stance focuses on the dynamic of the Spirit's leading and upon the responsibility of the disciples to walk in the Spirit. Here is the key for a global fellowship in which there can be a unity of the Spirit amidst divergence of cultures.

To walk in the resurrection is to live in hope. We who have experienced the new humanity Jesus is creating are affirming that this is the way of the future. We are declaring that the old is passing away, the new is come. Paul writes of "the hope laid up for you in heaven," asserting that it is "Christ in you, the hope of glory" (Colossians 1:5, 27). In 1 Thessalonians 5:8, 9 he says we guard the heart with faith and love and guard the mind with hope. Amidst the despair that grips many in the plight of mankind, amidst violence and war, suffering and starvation, anxiety and fear, the disciple shares the hope of the resurrection life. God has begun a work in history that He will not leave off until He achieves the goal. We stand in this hope. We serve in this hope. We are saved by this hope. We do not despair.

"If then you have been raised with Christ, seek the things that are above, where Christ is, seated at the right hand of God" (Colossians 3:1).

"Now may the God of peace, who brought again from the dead our Lord Jesus, the great shepherd of the sheep, by the blood of the eternal covenant, equip you with everything good that you may do his will, working in you that which is pleasing in his sight, through Jesus Christ; to whom be glory for ever and ever. Amen." (Hebrews 13:20, 21).

NOTES

Chapter 1. The Centrality of Christ

1. C. F. D. Moule, *The Significance of the Message of the Resurrection for Faith in Jesus Christ* (London: SCM Press, 1968), p. 98.
2. T. W. Manson, *The Teaching of Jesus* (New York: Cambridge University Press, 1951), p. 286.
3. Oscar Cullmann, *Salvation in History* (London: SCM Press, 1967).

Chapter 2. The Knowledge of God

1. Cullmann, *op. cit.* p. 16.
2. *Ibid.*, p. 65. See pp. 64-74 on the subject of hermeneutics.

Chapter 3. Understanding Oneself

1. Cecil Osborne, *The Art of Understanding Yourself* (Grand Rapids, Mich.: Zondervan, 1967), p. 29.
2. Keith Miller, *The Becomers* (Waco, Tex.: Word Books, 1973), pp. 115, 116.

Chapter 4. Experiencing Reconciliation

1. J. C. Wenger, *Even unto Death* (Richmond, Va.: John Knox, 1961), pp. 97-102.
2. Helmut Gollwitzer, *Die Revolution Des Reiches Gottes und die Gesellschaft* (München: Kösel Verlag, 1969), p. 142.
3. Paul Tournier, *Whole Persons in a Broken World* (New York: Harper and Row, 1964).

Chapter 5. A New Creation in Christ

1. Alan Walker, *Breakthrough: Rediscovery of the Holy Spirit* (Nashville, Tenn.: Abingdon Press, 1969), pp. 19-22.

Chapter 6. Walking in the Resurrection

1. John H. Yoder, ed., *The Legacy of Michael Sattler* (Scottdale, Pa.: Herald Press, 1973), pp. 34-43.
2. Soren Kierkegaard, *Training in Christianity* (Princeton, N.J.: Princeton University Press, 1957).

Chapter 7. Citizens of Christ's Kingdom

1. Yoder, *op. cit.*, p. 23.
2. Glenn Clark, *I Will Lift Up Mine Eyes* (New York: Harper and Row, 1937), p. 35.
3. *Ibid.*, p. 126.

4. See article in *The Mennonite Encyclopedia* (Scottdale, Pa.: Herald Press, 1955).
5. Cullmann, *op. cit.*, p. 311.
6. George Eldon Ladd, *The Gospel of the Kingdom* (Grand Rapids, Mich.: Eerdmans, 1971), p. 112.

Chapter 8. *The Church as a Community*

1. Osborne, *op. cit.*, 19.

Chapter 9. *The Missionary Principle*

1. Quoted by Donald Miller, *The Nature and Mission of the Church* (Richmond, Va.: John Knox, 1957), p. 69.
2. Statement made in a lecture, Theological Seminary, University of Basel, Winter Session, 1974.
3. Oscar Cullmann, *Salvation in History* (Chatham: SCM, W. & J. Mackey and Co., Ltd., 1967).
4. Elton Trueblood, *Alternative to Futility* (New York: Harper and Row, 1948).
5. See *Christianity Today*, February 1, 1974.

Chapter 10. *Relating to Government*

1. Mark O. Hatfield, "Repentance, Politics, and Power," in *The Post American*, January 1974.
2. Karl Menninger, *Whatever Became of Sin*? (New York: Hawthorn, 1973).
3. Carl F. H. Henry, *World Vision* magazine, January 1974, p. 17.
4. In an address on church-state relations, Eastern Mennonite College, Harrisonburg Va., 1967.
5. *The Complete Writings of Menno Simons, op. cit.*, p. 922.
6. Alan Walker, *Breakthrough* (Nashville, Tenn.: Abingdon Press, 1968), p. 76.
7. *The Complete Writings of Menno Simons, op. cit.*, pp. 554, 555.
8. *The Mennonite Encyclopedia, op. cit.*, Vol. II, p. 424.

Chapter 11. *God and Mammon*

1. William Temple, *Nature, Man, and God* (London: Macmillan, 1953).
2. *The Complete Writings of Menno Simons, op. cit.*, (from his tract, "The New Birth"), p. 94.
3. Matthew 6:25-34. See my work on the Sermon on the Mount, *The Expanded Life* (Nashville, Tenn.: Abingdon Press, 1972).
4. *The Mennonite Encyclopedia*, Vol. IV, *op. cit.*, p. 600.
5. In the *Post American*, January 1974, p. 7.

Chapter 12. *Led by the Spirit of Jesus*

1. See my book, *Quench Not the Spirit* (Scottdale, Pa.: Herald Press, 1961 and 1975).

THE AUTHOR

Myron S. Augsburger is President and Professor of Theology of Eastern Mennonite College and Seminary, Harrisonburg, Virginia. He has lectured on many college and university campuses as a Staley Distinguished Christian Scholar.

He serves on the board of administration of the National Association of Evangelicals, as well as on the boards of the Council for the Advancement of Small Colleges, the President's Board of the Christian College Consortium, the Shenandoah Valley Educational Television Corporation, and the Presbyterian Ministers Fund.

Born in Elida, Ohio, Augsburger was ordained to the Christian ministry in 1951 as pastor of Tuttle Avenue Mennonite Church, Sarasota, Florida. During the past quarter century he has served as evangelist with Inter-Church Evangelism, Inc., Harrisonburg, Virginia. His community-wide crusades and congregational renewal meetings have taken him across the United States and Canada, as well as into Jamaica, India, the Middle East, the Orient, Africa, and Central America.

Augsburger has engaged in postgraduate study at the University of Basel, Basel, Switzerland; the University of Michigan, Ann Arbor, Michigan; and George Washington University, Washington, D.C. He earned his ThD and ThM degrees at Union Theological Seminary, Richmond, Virginia, his BD at Goshen Biblical Seminary, Elkhart, Indiana and his ThB and BA degrees at Eastern Mennonite College and Seminary.

He is author of *Called to Maturity, Quench Not the Spirit, Plus Living, Invitation to Discipleship, Principles of Biblical Interpretation, Pilgrim Aflame, Faith for a Secular World, The Broken Chalice, The Expanded Life*, and *Perspective on Missions in the Orient*. His publishers include Herald Press, Bethany Fellowship, Abingdon Press, Word Books, and Progress Press.

Myron Augsburger and his wife, Esther (Kniss), are the parents of two married sons, John and Michael, and a daughter, Marcia.